The Ten Symptoms of Enlightenment:

A Practical Guide To Your Newly Awakened Self

by
James F. Twyman
with
Stephen J. Kosmyna

Books by James F. Twyman

The Moses Code

The Barn Dance

Emissary of Light

Emissary of Love

Giovanni and the Camino of St. Francis

I AM Wishes Fulfilled Meditation

(with Dr. Wayne Dyer)

The Kabbalah Code: A True Adventure

(with Philip Gruber)

Love, God, and the Art of French Cooking

Messages From Thomas

The Prayer of St. Francis

Praying Peace

The Proof

(with Anakha Coman)

The Proposing Tree

St. Francis and the Animals Who Loved Him

The Secret of the Beloved Disciple

Ten Spiritual Lessons I Learned at the Mall

Touching the Divine

The Impersonal Light: Journey into I AM Consciousness

The Nondual Universe — The Spirituality of Enlightenment Made Simple for the Western World

The Jeshua Code

ISBN: 9798844216206 (Paperback)

Table of Contents

Introduction

The Ten Symptoms of Enlightenment is the first in a series I am calling major/minor books. Though short and concise (you could easily read any of them in one or two sittings) they are of major importance and value. We have all heard the saying: "You can't judge a book by its cover." In this case, you can't judge a book by how many pages it has. I feel this is true for The Ten Symptoms of Enlightenment.

You were probably attracted to the title of this short book because you sense something changing in your life. Perhaps the change is subtle, and yet for others, it will feel dramatic or even catastrophic. There might be physical changes occurring in your body or mind, or you might be feeling the need to dramatically change your life. That being said, here is the question I hope you will answer as you begin reading Ten Symptoms:

Is it possible that you are experiencing the early stages of enlightenment?

I have met hundreds of people over the years who felt the weight of this question but had no one to turn to for guidance. Their attraction to the things of this world and everything they once held dear was shifting, sometimes like an earthquake beneath their feet, and they wondered if something was wrong. There was no one there to say "nothing is wrong, just the opposite — something is very right." Knowing that this is a natural stage of the awakening could have helped tremendously. Perhaps it will help you. This is my hope as I begin to write this important book.

You now have a friend who has gone through the stages of this awakening and is ready to take your hand and guide you toward calm waters. Don't worry about *believing* anything at this stage. Belief will only get you so far. What we are concerned with is KNOWING the truth, or having a feeling of certainty that transcends this world. Belief is of the mind but certainty is a quality of the soul, and that is where we are pointed together. So do your best to give up all your judgments and concerns about what is or is not happening, or even what stage of awakening you are at. Just know that you are ready to step into a vast new world that will be very, very different than anything you have ever known before.

That is all you need for now — to know that you are ready for this.

My awakening was quickened in 1995 when I was introduced to a group of mystics living in the forests along the border of Croatia and Bosnia called The Emissaries of Light. They claimed to have been present in different parts of the world for hundreds, even thousands of years, usually in areas that were experiencing great violence. This was near the end of the Balkan war during the collapse of Yugoslavia and I was there performing a series of peace concerts. I was escorted to the area where the Emissary community was hidden and I spent several days with them. My first book, Emissary of Light, came from that experience. I learned many things while I was with the community, but there was one lesson the Emissaries taught me that was of supreme importance, something for each one of us to learn and accept. They said:

"Tell everyone that they're ready."

Of course, I asked the obvious next question: "Ready for what?"

"Ready for everything...to see what has always been seen and to know what has always

3

been known. Tell everyone you meet that there's nothing left to DO. It's time to simply BE the Truth and has always been True."

And that is what I have tried to do for nearly three decades. Every book I have written and every lesson I have shared has this message at its core. And now I am here to share that message with you. The only thing that remains is for you to either receive or reject what you hear. My suggestion, even if it is still a bit of a stretch, is to be willing to consider the possibility that I know what I am sharing here. All you need to do is allow the door to be cracked open, and if you feel comfortable doing that, everything in your life will change, not for the better, but the best!

So, if you have felt these shifts and changes happening in your life, you have come to the right place. Take your time reading these words and most of all — stay open.

Are You Enlightened Now?

When you hear the word *enlightenment*, what do you think of? Do you imagine Indian gurus sitting in caves meditating, or perhaps historic religious leaders like the Buddha or Jesus? One thing you probably don't imagine when you think about what it means to be enlightened is yourself. It might happen to other people but certainly not to you. There is an image you hold in your mind, probably someone who never has negative or divisive thoughts, who has a continual radiant smile and exudes an energy of perfect stillness and grace.

"That certainly isn't me," you are likely thinking. "I have negative thoughts all the time, and I'm no one special."

Ah, and here is the main image we hold when we think of someone enlightened — they are special. They are not the ordinary lot, someone who has issues to deal with and problems to solve. They lift above such concerns as if they have wings, and their feet never touch the ground.

I am going to encourage you to throw away all those images. All they do is separate you from the simple truth this book aims to deliver. And here it is:

You are enlightened NOW

Enlightenment simply means filled with light, and it describes you, *and* me, *and* everyone else in the world no matter what they think of themselves or how they handle the issues and problems that come into their lives. The first thought many will have when they read those words is: "What about Hitler…was he filled with light?" Hitler is the poster boy for evil, and he, of all people, seems to have lost any radiance he ever possessed. You might believe that there is a point at which our actions negate the light within, never to return.

This is not what I believe at all. Unless I unconditionally choose to see the light instead of the shadow, or grace instead of sin, I will inevitably fall into the trap of judgment and error. Ego-mind loves this. It looks for exceptions to God's law, and Hitler is the most convenient target. When Neale Donald Walsch was deep in his conversation with God (in the book <u>Conversations With God</u>) he was told that Hitler went to Heaven, and many people used that as an excuse to throw the book into the trash. But for others, this was the point at which ego's need to look for an exception dissolved and they were suddenly able to recognize what we have always suspected was true — God's love is unconditional, and we have been called to the same standard.

There is a section in <u>A Course In Miracle</u>, the most inspirational book I have ever read, that describes this perfectly:

"Those who seek the light are merely
covering their eyes. The light is in them
now. Enlightenment is but a recognition,
not a change at all." (ACIM Lesson 188)

You don't need to change anything to know that you are filled with light. All you need to do is remove the blocks that are covering that light. And that is why you are reading this book — to identify and dissolve all those blocks and barriers, then come into a full, unchallengeable experience of your own Divinity.

In 1999 I was invited to speak at a spiritual conference in Holland and I decided to bring my 14-year-old daughter, Angela, with me. The conference was sponsored by a man who was the perfect image of an enlightened guru, or at least what most people would imagine one was. He was from India, had a long dark beard and spoke in very soft tones, so soft it was often hard to hear what he was saying. I remember walking about thirty feet behind this man when a woman said to her friend: "I can't believe we're walking so close to the master." I wanted to grab her arm and say something like: "He's no different from you...the light is shining in you just as bright." If I said those words she probably would have looked at me as if I lost my mind. It is easy to attribute such qualities to someone who plays or looks the part, but once again, the idea that the light shines equally bright in each one of us is often hard to accept.

I was scheduled to deliver a talk the next afternoon. It was a huge conference, with about 1000 people sitting silently in a dark theater. There was no talking and certainly no laughter. This was a serious group and I wondered if there was a way I could lighten things up a bit while delivering a transformative message. When it was my turn to speak I stood in front of the group, looked around for a few seconds, then said: "You are all taking yourselves way too seriously." The crowd erupted with laughter. Thank God, because they could have booed me off the stage. Then I began sharing, basically the same message I am sharing right now.

I told stories to show how we are all an extension of God's love, and the extension of God's love never leaves its source. I explained that each one of us is perfect and whole exactly as we are, and it is only when we accept that fact that the dysfunctional beliefs that have held us back begin falling away. I was funny and I told my stories well. Or at least I thought I had.

My daughter was anxious to leave and get back to London where she was having much more fun. An hour or so after I was finished with my talk we were walking toward the door to catch a bus back to the airport when a woman stopped us. She said that there was something very important she had to share and she would not let me leave until she had the chance. Angela pulled at my arm as if to say to forget her, but I couldn't do it. I stopped and asked her what she needed to say.

"I came to this conference because I've read your books and I've listened to your interviews, and I could tell from everything I read and heard that you are a holy man."

I looked at my daughter and watched her roll her eyes. This was the last thing she wanted to hear, someone telling her dad how holy he is.

"Around an hour ago you took the stage and I was overjoyed," she continued. "I was finally getting the chance to listen to this great man I admire so much and have learned so many things from. That's when you looked out at the audience and said that we were being far too serious. And it was in that moment that I realized something, something I never would have expected before."

She paused and I looked into her eyes. She could have said anything at that point. Perhaps she finally realized that the light within her was just as bright as it is in me or anyone else...something along those lines. But then she took a breath and said:

"I realized that I was completely disappointed."

This is when my daughter lost it. She covered her mouth and turned away so the woman wouldn't see how much she was enjoying what she just heard. I looked at the woman and asked:

"Why were you disappointed?"

"As I said," she explained, "I've read all your books and could tell you are a holy man, but when you were on the stage you were funny and whimsical, and it took me by surprise. You spoke in a way that was so ordinary and I could see myself in everything you were describing. And that's when I realized that you are not holy at all…in fact…"

That is when I interrupted her. "You realized that I'm no different from you."

"Exactly," she exclaimed in a loud voice. "How could you be holy when you are no different from me?"

And that is when I asked her the question that might have changed her life if she was able to hear.

"What I'm wondering is this — who were you disappointed in? Me or yourself?"

She looked like the air was suddenly sucked out of her lungs. She walked away, probably more disappointed than she was before. What she didn't realize was that I had given her a great gift. I was hoping she would see the illusions she held in her mind about how an enlightened person should act, what they should say and how serious they would be, especially when hundreds of people were watching. Instead, I did something she didn't expect:

I was myself!

I refused to play the *Enlightened Teacher* game with her. All it did was amplify her belief that she was not filled with light, or enlightened because the person she had placed high on a pedestal — me — was no different from her. She had the chance to throw away all the stories she had read about enlightened teachers living in caves high in the Himalayan mountains, or mystics who could endure extreme heat or cold without the slightest grimace on their faces. She was being confronted with the most important lesson she could ever learn — that she was holy and wholly loved by God exactly as she was.

And now you are being confronted with the same lesson. Are you ready to realize that you don't need to change to be filled with light, to be enlightened? And here is the best thing: when you finally do accept this, everything changes on its own. There will be no effort involved, no mountains to climb or obstacles to overcome. You will finally be able to relax and realize that your essence is love, itself. You will finally discover that the truth within you has never been challenged by the dream of separation and that nothing is blocking you from receiving the love you deserve.

You will finally recognize who you really are, and you will see the same face of holiness on everyone you meet.

A Quick Personal Check-In

Let us pause for a moment and take a short quiz. Answer these questions and keep track of how many yeses you score.

1. Have you been feeling a shift in your consciousness that makes you feel disconnected from the world you have always known and the life you have always lived?

2. Is it hard for you to hold your thoughts together as you once did, or maintain steady control over your mind?

3. Do you find yourself wanting to simplify your life and live without the distractions of unnecessary possessions or responsibilities?

4. Has your need for social interaction diminished, replaced by a stronger desire for meditative stillness?

5. Do you experience unexpected rushes of love for people you have never met before?

6. Have you sensed unusual and powerful sensations in your heart area, your forehead, or the top of your head?

7. Has your need to be right when interacting with others decreased?

8. Does the phrase *"I am happy even when I'm not"* apply to you?

9. Has your concept of God loosened and relaxed, becoming a gentle recognition of the Divine in every moment?

10. Do you spend more time looking at flowers, clouds, children, or puppies than ever before?

If you answered *Yes* to eight or more of these questions, you are probably experiencing the early stages of enlightenment. Don't worry, there is no cure for this condition. You can try to reverse the process and go back to your former attachments, but the pain will be too great. You have peeked out from beneath the blanket too far and any attempt to go back to sleep will result in dreams you don't want to experience.

Speaking of dreams…

Have you ever slept a few hours longer than you are accustomed to and your dreams start to become disjointed and terrifying? Why do you think this happens? It is your mind screaming "wake up, you have been sleeping too long." There comes a point where sleep becomes unhelpful and waking up to start your day becomes a requirement.

I am going to take a giant leap and hope you can stay with me. This may be hard to grasp at the moment, but if you answered *Yes* to eight or more of our questions you will likely feel a subtle, or even powerful, reaction to my next statement:

"This is exactly what is happening to you individually, and to the world you perceive, right now. You have been asleep too long and the chaos of the world has increased to the point that you will not be able to stand it. In other words, the dream of separation is about to come to a dramatic end!"

What do you feel right now? Does this statement make sense or does it sound like a load of nonsense? Here is my advice: If it sounds like baloney, close the book and throw it in the trash. You are not ready. I don't mean that negatively, only that there are still desires and attachments you need to work through, things you should go through before you come to the point of no return.

You will come to that point sooner or later, I promise. It is inevitable, which is the good news. It means that at some point, maybe a minute from now or eighteen years in the future, you are going to look around yourself and say "this isn't working like it used to…I need more…I need something deeper." Then you will order this book again because a light has been ignited in your soul and you remember that the information in these pages offered something you need, something that shatters the world you thought you lived in and all the desires you once held.

Then you will be ready!

This short book is an owner's manual for those who find themselves in the early stages of waking up. That is my preferred way to describe the process — waking up — rather than words like "enlightenment" or "spiritual illumination". Did you know that there is a way to realize with total certainty that you are fully awake? Here it is:

When you achieve full enlightenment you will look around at everyone you see, or even think of, and you will perceive them as filled with light…NO MATTER WHAT they say, how they act, or how asleep they seem. In other words, an enlightened being sees only other enlightened beings. Period!

How close are you to this? Are you able to look past all the silly mistakes people make and see them as whole, complete, and filled with light? Maybe you find yourself in the early stage of this way of *seeing*, able to see the light in some people but not everyone. That is fine. Don't put any pressure on yourself. All you need is the willingness to SEE. A little willingness is all you need to burn away everything you no longer need and let the fire reveal the Truth that has always been True.

You are going to see that line many times in this book: *The Truth that has always been True.* Experiencing this Truth is the essence of what it means to be awake. What is in the Mind of God remains as it has always been — perfect, whole, and complete. There is no interruption to this perfection; there is no change to this wholeness, and there is nothing in the world that can challenge the fact that you have everything you need right here and now to awaken to what we call The Real World. Once you have experienced this reality you will never fall into ego's dream of separation again.

Let me put it as simply as I can — you are here to learn to See as God Sees, to Love as God Loves, and to Know what God Knows. What does God See? God sees only God, or wholeness. What does God Love? Since God is the very essence of love, it is the only thing God can do — Love unconditionally. And what does God Know? God knows that *only Love is real*. Therefore, God looks past all the illusions and dreams that have captured your mind (until now) and sees only the Truth shining in eternal light.

And now, at last, you are beginning to experience this for yourself. This book will help you recognize this reality, then help you abide in the experience of being awake. But there is something you should realize right from the beginning — waking up to the Truth that has always been True takes work. This is mind training, and though it is sometimes the most joyful training you will ever experience, it requires an unwavering commitment to challenging everything you believe about yourself, the people you see around you, and the world you live in. If you are willing to enter this classroom and do the required course work, then... "Kansas is about to go bye-bye."

19

But don't be fooled by the word *joyful*. You will remember in the quiz the question: *Does the phrase "I am happy even when I'm not" apply to you?* This will be challenging work, training your mind to think and perceive in a completely new way. It is not for the spiritual tourist, or someone looking for a way to make themselves feel better about their life. If anything, this information will shake the very core of your life and will challenge every belief you have ever held about yourself and the world. And yet, even at its most challenging stages, it will be joyful because you will know that you are breaking free from what I call the *gravitational pull of ego* into the experience of Divine Weightlessness. Imagine that for a moment, coming to a stage of your life where you are no longer limited by the same laws that you claimed till now, and that claimed you. You have lifted above it all, and even though it took enormous energy to get you there, there is no way you will ever return to your former life.

So let us look at the Ten Symptoms of Enlightenment. Like any other symptom, they indicate that something is changing, or something is about to happen. If you start to feel the symptoms of a cold it means you should stop what you are doing, drink lots of fluids and get more rest. If you don't your symptoms may increase. In this case, noticing the symptoms of enlightenment will help you navigate your way through the inevitable changes in your life and enter the experience of wholeness with little to no resistance. Read these through and see which ones apply to your life.

The 10 Symptoms of Enlightenment

1.   **Worldly indifference:** Things of the world that once satisfied you now lack vibrancy and attraction.

2.   **A profound shift in desire:** Former desires have fallen away, reduced to only one — to swim in the ocean of love.

3.   **Depth of interaction:** Every encounter you have with another, no matter how mundane, feels holy and blessed.

4.   **A sense of inaction:** The need to DO anything has been replaced by the desire to BE everything.

5.   **A Feeling of timelessness:** Time loses its meaning and importance; only the present moment matters.

6.   **Attachment to special relationships has diminished:** Every person you meet is the Beloved in disguise, replacing the desire to elevate certain relationships above others.

7.   **Concern about personal well-being has decreased:** As the concept of separation decreases you are released from individual needs and desires

8.   **Tenderness for all beings:** The desire to serve increases, including a sense of love and connection with the smallest and most vulnerable creatures.

9.   **Concrete perceptual thoughts start to fade:** Your thoughts are becoming more abstract as the space between your thoughts increases.

10.   **The need to define the symptoms of enlightenment disappears:** The concept of unenlightened has fallen away, replaced by a feeling of unity and wholeness.

Now that you know the symptoms of being awake, let us examine them one by one. Each of these experiences is common, though each person will progress through them at their own pace and to different degrees. For example, you may notice that your thoughts are becoming more abstract with greater space between each one, but you are still feeling the desire for a partner, or a special relationship. You may relate to seven or eight of these symptoms but not to everyone. Remember, no two people will move into an enlightened or awakened state in the same way or at the same speed. These are benchmarks, and they are certainly not written in stone. Use them as you will and receive the help they offer. At the end of this book, we will offer simple steps for integration, helping you to move even deeper into the experience of your awakening.

Symptom #1:

Worldly Indifference

Things of the world that once satisfied you now lack vibrancy and attraction.

The first symptom of enlightenment is worldly indifference. Things of the world that once satisfied you now lack the attraction you once experienced.

Try to remember a time in your life when you found great satisfaction in pursuing the things of the physical world. Maybe it was pursuing a career or a promotion you have been hoping to receive. Or perhaps you worked hard to earn enough money to buy a car, then after you finally achieved your goal you got into the vehicle and smelled the new car aroma and you felt deep satisfaction.

But, after a few weeks, or maybe less, the new car aroma began to fade and that same feeling of "wanting" returned. What changed, the car or something deeper inside? Have you noticed that the desire to achieve things in the world has decreased, or that you don't find as much vibrancy or energy as you once did?

This is what we mean when we refer to worldly indifference. It is a feeling that the world you see holds nothing that you really, really want.

When we use the word *want* in this context, we think of it with a capital "W" as opposed to a small "w". There are always things that you want and need: a roof over your head or food on your table. These are small "w" wants. But there are also things that you want with a capital "W", or what you really, really want. These are the qualities of the Soul — love, compassion, grace. See if you can identify a few of these qualities, then ask yourself this question:

"Will the world I see give that to me? Has it ever offered such deep satisfaction?"

If you are honest with yourself, you may notice that the world has never given you what it claims or what it promises. Maybe you have come to the point where you can no longer follow the rules of the world. This is when you know that you are approaching the first symptom of enlightenment — worldly indifference.

A profound shift in priorities has taken place where you are no longer looking outside for something that can only be found within. You have arrived at a critical stage, and this is why it is the first symptom of living an enlightened life or waking up from the illusion you have lived under for so long. You are waking up into reality itself. There is nothing in this world that can compare with this experience.

So when you begin to feel this indifference, go with it. Don't try to change it or run away. Wrap your arms around the feeling and let it take you wherever it wants to take you. I promise that it will lead you to an experience that you can not even imagine, a place that is so new and so bright that the world you were once so attracted to will begin to fade on its own.

The world you thought was so important begins to lose its shine and the light you suddenly feel reveals the real world, the world that your Soul perceives. So, when you get to this point of experiencing a lack of attraction or a lack of vibrancy in the world, know that this is the first step in your awakening. Don't try and go back and don't try to cover your eyes because you have come to the point where you will no longer be able to hide again.

The shadows where you used to hide will not be able to contain you. Hiding isn't even an option at this point. You have finally dipped your toe in this water of true light and this pool of enlightenment is calling you to be ALL IN.

As you begin experiencing this first symptom, you may even think something is wrong with you. You may be asking yourself, "Why have I lost my passion and appetite for the things of this world?" Instead of thinking something is wrong, know at a deep level that something is right in a profound and extraordinarily beautiful way.

As the bud of the rose unfurls in its desire to take in more life, so is your very essence calling for recognition of its desire to live in the light of truth.

You are beginning to move into your new home, though you never realized that this is the home you always longed for. As you decide to move in, you recognize this is the house where tranquility has been living and the place from where your Soul has been calling you.

The infinite greets you at the door and you immediately feel the spaciousness of your new residence. A sense of warmth and freedom washes over you. Here understanding begins to rush in. You feel an energy that is inclusive of love, and you see that this new place is furnished with wisdom and filled with true light.

As you continue to awaken, you will notice that the longing and discontent that were your constant companions begin to fade and drift away. You have finally made it home and that former insatiable desire can only be satisfied by living here.

Congratulations. You have entered the Kingdom. You look with amazement upon your new home and realize that your enlightenment has begun!

However, as with any symptom, we must proceed with caution. At this early stage, our symptoms are positive in nature indicating that there is something much more desirable waiting for us; something wonderful that has always been there within us calling us home. As we move through our new estate, we may notice that some other symptoms arise that are negative in nature. We are exploring and we are feeling good as we investigate every nook and cranny, discovering what is here for us, yet there remains a pull in the opposite direction. We may feel like there is something else still tugging at us trying to draw us away.

Since fear doesn't live here, we dive deeper, unafraid, and find that ego has slid in through the door right behind us. Your ego doesn't want you to live here. It feels threatened so it works to pull you back into the old familiar comfort zone of what once was. But you have come too far. You can not *not* know what you know now.

Ego only influences us as we give our attention to it and continue to feed it. We must remain vigilant. We may love our new place absolutely, but since we are creatures of habit — habitual in thought, word, and action — the worldly desires simply do not vanish all at once. It has become a habit to want the things we thought we wanted. Even the belief that something is missing and these attractions might provide us with some relief, even this has become a habit of belief. This is why it is so important to stand guard, watch your thoughts, and be careful about what we allow into our consciousness. Energy flows where our attention goes.

When you look at this from the perspective of consciousness, you are shifting into a new frequency. You have adjusted the dial so to speak.

The world in which you once lived is being left behind and your ego doesn't like this one bit.

We could make the comparison to a dial on the radio as you travel from one city to another. Let us say that where you used to live — the temporal, the worldly, rooted in an ego dominant consciousness — is represented by an all-negative news talk station. As you come into range of your new home the station begins to change as you adjust the frequency with your radio dial. Let us say your new sacred home is represented by classical music or a smooth jazz station. You keep turning the dial until you find the frequency of what you truly want to hear. As you are leaving one city and approaching another, you often experience static and fuzziness, a lack of clarity as one station fades away and another comes into range.

You can make a conscious choice here. You can choose to keep the dial on the same negative news radio, searching until you find another that is in range, or you can seek out the classical or smooth jazz station. Likewise, as you move about your new home and are confronted with the lurking ego, you can make a choice similar to what you did with your radio dial. You can choose to remain in your new dwelling place, or you can bow to ego's insistence that you leave, returning to the world that never really satisfied you. You always have a choice.

Ego's cries often grow louder as you come to realize that this new dwelling place — this kingdom of heaven here and now — is what you wanted all along. Stay with this blissful feeling because, to remove habitual thoughts, you must replace them with something else. Ego feeds on habit; it is where it is most comfortable because it is so familiar. Here, feeling is the secret. Your Soul knows where home is. Your Soul has not lost its awareness of your divinity. Feel the truth of that. Know and feel that your essence is of God, that you are one of God. Know and feel how good it is to know that there is only one Life, that Life is God, and that Life is your life and your home now. Stay with this. Ego will soon become submissive to your holy, sacred spiritual essence.

You may be saying or thinking, "OK, I get it, but there is still a lot that I want to be, do, and have and I'm not sure it's ego or my soul. What if it's the will of God?"

This question most likely comes up for everyone at this stage of awakening as you move into your new place in higher consciousness. You have received some very simple and specific instructions regarding this from the greatest Master Teacher who has ever walked this earth.

He said that we should always "Seek first the Kingdom of God" and that is exactly what you are doing here. You are moving into this kingdom of enlightenment, this new dwelling place, to abide always in the Light of Goodness and Grace, abandoning everything else so that you might fully enter.

One very illuminating thing is the word "seek". In our human experience, we rarely go in search of something unless we know that it exists, even though it may be hidden somewhere. When we were children, we might have played a game called hide and seek. We all know the objective of this game — to go in search of something or someone we know is out there, somewhere, yet in hiding, concealed from our five senses. This game would not be very fun to play if we knew that what we were looking for didn't exist.

It is the same on the path of awakening. We know true light is always shining, we know the Kingdom is within us. Our Soul has been calling to us from the very breadth, depth, and height of the Kingdom from the moment we started drifting away. Ego has worked very hard to conceal and muffle this voice of our Soul, yet we still hear it because it is coming from the core of who we think we are. Returning home is the only thing that will satisfy us now.

Now back to the question about whether there is still a lot you want to be, do, and have. If you would look back to the Master Teacher and his instruction, you will find that he reveals the answer when you look at his complete statement. Here it is and here we find the assurance he offers that answers this question; "Seek first the kingdom of God and His righteousness, and then all these things will be given to you too." This is a simple declaration of cause and effect. He says that if we seek, everything that is good will be added to us. This is what we call The Good News.

We let it all go. We seek only to fully enter what was always our home, the Kingdom. This is our awakening. We release all sense of strain, of trying and striving, of going and getting, of plotting and scheming; and all that satisfies most completely is simply given to us through grace.

I invite you to think for a moment about the things you think you want or have wanted throughout your life. Have you ever taken the time to sit with these desires and ask yourself why you want them? Answering the why will reveal the true nature of your desire. You will very clearly see if it is ego wanting to lift itself higher, or a worthy ideal born of love that serves and shines the Divine Light you are in truth. Go into your room, shut the door, and retreat from the sensual world. Knock, ask, and seek the answer to your "why". It is only when your eyes are closed that you will see all that you already are and that which is yours to reveal.

Other simple questions to ask as you examine your desires are these:

- Is this what Love would want?
- Is this what Love would do?
- Is this what Love would seek to be?
- Is this what Love would seek to have?
- Is this what Love would seek to give?

Identifying, exploring, considering, and sorting through these things as you experience this first symptom should move you to a place of profound clarity. You now know with certainty, beyond a shadow of a doubt, that you are on the right track. You are moving back home. You have chosen to live in and from the Light, from your very Soul, which is the holy, sacred presence of God pressing out into visibility as you, the Real you, Divine and wholly whole.

All that is yours to do now is guard your thoughts by following the advice of another great teacher from days gone by. His name was Paul and he suggested that whatever is true, whatever is honorable, whatever is just, whatever is pure, whatever is lovely, whatever is gracious — if there is any excellence and if there is anything worthy of praise — think about these things. And as you fill your mind and meditate on these things you will complete your move into your new home, discovering more joy than you ever thought possible because this is where joy lives.

Let us keep moving forward and become mindful of the other symptoms you may experience as you come to understand your newly awakened Self.

Symptom #2:

A Profound Shift in Desire

Former desires have fallen away, reduced to only one – to swim in the ocean of love.

Do you remember when you were a child and Christmas was approaching? Maybe a catalog arrived in the mail and you spent days paging through it, marking all the things you hoped to receive on Christmas morning. You probably made a list and took it with you to the mall or shopping center, then sat on Santa Claus's lap where you shared the litany of toys, games, and treasures you longed for.

But something has shifted regarding that longing. It isn't as strong as it used to be. Maybe you look at a catalog or search Google, or any of the pages and websites that once brought you such joy, but now you feel only emptiness. The stuff that once filled your house feels like weights holding you down. You are no longer seeking after more goods but a higher level of goodness, both for you and everyone around you.

This is how you know that you have entered the second stage of enlightenment; when you feel this profound shift in your desire. All roads lead to this one — your longing to swim in the ocean of love. It is almost impossible to identify what you are feeling, but you know everything has changed. The things that were once so valuable have lost their shine and your sights are set on something higher than what you can receive from this world.

Now that you know what is really happening, you find yourself filled with joy. What seemed like a problem is now seen as a solution. You may not have even realized that there was a problem, but your longing for goodness and the higher qualities of the soul begin to overwhelm your consciousness. It also becomes increasingly difficult to spend time with people who have not reached this stage. Maybe you are shopping with a friend and their enthusiasm to buy half the store fills you with a feeling of confusion and dread.

Be patient with these others. They'll be where you are soon enough. Sometimes we need to run out the clock before we are ready to shift to a higher frequency. Your patience with them will lead to greater patience for yourself.

So give the gift you would like to receive. You did not arrive at this place alone, but through the help and efforts of many other people, whether they realized they were helping you or not. Just keep your focus on that ocean of love you feel moving within you. Dive into the river and let the current of love take you, drawing you effortlessly to that infinite space. The shift you are feeling is a shift into a new life and a new way of being. But at the same time, it is very ancient because it is the final identification with your True Self. So relax and be patient. You are beginning to wake up from the dream of separation, and everything is now seen in light.

The dramatic shift you feel in this stage is where the intuitive urge for growth and expansion gains momentum. Your worldly desires have fallen away because you are focused on fully moving into this place. You have decided to stay and settle into this new home where love lives. It feels so good here, so natural because you notice that everything is made of Love — including you.

In this stage of enlightenment, the awareness of the Love you are replaces every concept and idea that came before. You realize that you have begun feeling less of the gravitational pull of ego and more of the Divine Weightlessness I mentioned earlier. You continue to awaken and as your eyes open you realize that the Truth is everything you are, everything you are made of, and the very fiber and substance of your being. Of course, this Truth is Love Itself.

You are and have always been this Love but you allow yourself to drift away whenever you think about that which you are not, and chances are you have spent a great deal of time drifting, thinking about that which you are not. As you begin to fully awaken you will want to pay attention to the words that follow every I Am statement you make, both silently and out loud.

While spiritually asleep you may have claimed many things for yourself that were not true. How often have you thought or said: I am not good enough; I am not smart enough; I am not worthy? You may have thought: I am this body I find myself in; or I am this place where I live; I am this job I perform; I am what I think; I am this emotion or even; I am this dis-ease. Spend some time in the silence and ask yourself why you allowed yourself to drift away like this. Your constant focus on the *you* that you see in the mirror has led to nothing but confusion. Your physical self is not what you are!

Here and now, moving along this path of enlightenment, you move into the realization of what you TRULY are. You are Love! You now know you are Love. You can no longer *not* know this. Therefore, as you fully establish yourself in this stage, you will spend less time drifting away.

You have come to the point where you realize that love is all there is and all that is real. You then ask yourself:

"Why would I want anything less than what love is?"

"Why would I want to be anything that is not love?"

"Why would I want to do anything that is not born of love?"

You are also coming to know that God and Love are the same thing!

Another wise teacher named John said:

*"Whoever does not love does not know
God, because God is love." 1 John 4:8*

When you open your heart and mind to this there is no turning back. You would not want to if you could. From your limited human perspective, it may be difficult to say and claim:

"I Am the holy sacred presence of God."

Say those words out loud and see how they feel. It feels really good, doesn't it? Just remember when you are feeling good, you are feeling God and you are exactly where you should be — knowing your Truth.

You are God's Love in good times and in bad, in tough times and when the going is easy. And the love of God never decreases. God as unconditional love is always on and present everywhere with the same intensity, and this includes within your very Soul. The only thing that changes is the level and degree of awareness of this love you claim.

It is you who makes the choice consciously or unconsciously to falsely give power to something else in your human experience, whatever you perceive as greater than the Love God and the Love you are. Reading these words, if you would reflect on them for a moment, you would see how preposterous this is. That is why you are here, experiencing this symptom.

Make time to be still and know that you are adrift in a sea of love rather than being the fish that asks "what water?" You decide here and now to ceaselessly affirm:

"The holy sacred presence of Love is wholly present in me and as me. I Am the holy, sacred Presence of Love. I Am that, I Am."

What you are is God, pressing out as Love. This may be hard to wrap your head around, especially if you have had a traditional upbringing centered on the fundamentals of religiosity and the belief in separation. Love will free you from all those false beliefs and your own self-imposed limitations.

Allow your thoughts, your words, and actions to be rooted and grounded in Love. Remember, it is what you are made of anyway. Here at this stage, you finally abandon trying to be something you are not. This may feel uncomfortable at first because, if you are like most people, you probably have spent most of your life living it as something different from what you are in Truth. Before your awakening began you put on the same garment of the flesh day in and day out and lived in the clothing, or perhaps metal armor, that was not made from love. This is the outer you, the façade you have decided to shed at this stage of enlightenment.

It is important to point out that there are some side effects you may experience with this symptom as you navigate your way, swimming in this ocean of love.

As the tide moves in you will feel that there is nowhere you can go where the undertow of Love is not present. You have allowed yourself to be drawn in. Swimming here is most delightful. Without really noticing, your former desires have drifted away. You haven't noticed because they've been replaced by what Love wants to experience which is more Love. Specifically, Love desires to give itself away. This is its very nature: GIVE.

No need to worry because there is an infinite abundance of Love to draw from because Love knows no lack or limitation. The more you participate in giving Love away, the more you will have the experience of more Love rushing in. You will even feel a very pleasurable increase in the intensity of Love that is replenishing you. Rather than being obsessed with worldly desires, you will be preoccupied with the ways and means of distribution as you perpetually consider the actions you might take to share what you have finally discovered to be the real you — Love Itself.

You will finally discover how Love is a noun and a verb all at the same time. Initially, you will feel the warmth that Love provides as you realize that Love is what you are. Moving deeper into this stage you will become much more aware of the many dimensions of being that Love loves to explore. You will find that the very nature of Love gives, responds, attracts, engages, and moves in and through all that is, as an energy supporting life, selfless compassion, and understanding. Don't be alarmed. You are, perhaps for the first time, coming into an absolute knowing that only Love is real. As you finally adjust to wearing your garment of Love you will also realize that Love can behave in only one way. This is good and this is God — and you are THAT.

Another side effect you will notice is that the very nature that Love cannot separate from your nature. You are beginning to discover more of the infinite aspects of Love and the ways it can be expressed. This becomes easier and easier as you embody all that Love is by simply sharing, being, and radiating the Love you are. This is your primary desire and focus, here and now.

As you move about in this ocean of Love, you will automatically begin to see where you can apply this Love you are. You will very naturally want to sprinkle it everywhere. Don't hesitate in doing this. What is happening, so beautifully, so naturally, is the expansion into your Divine Self. Seeing how magnificently responsive everything is to the love you bring will serve to encourage you along your way. You will know beyond a shadow of a doubt that you matter. At this point, if you have not fully accepted that you are Love, the response you witness will serve as confirmation. You are now seeing how you can be what Love is and do what Love does which is so much more than just doing loving things. It is EVERYTHING at once.

One of the most beautiful side effects you are beginning to experience is the way everyone and everything looks as you see things through the lens of Love. This is a phenomenon everyone experiences as they move into an enlightened state of being. You will probably want to spend more time in nature as colors become more vibrantly alive, delicious, and fragrant. You may even begin to wonder, "Where has this beautiful world been?" It is all good, it is all God. Keep moving, keep being, keep living, loving, and swimming in this ocean of love. Take it all in from Love's perspective. It is truly amazing as you take in all that Life is.

You are discovering how everything responds to the energy that Love is and that you are. You will notice how perceptive even plants and animals are to the Love you are radiating. Like throwing a pebble in a pond and causing ripples, you, being aware of the Love you are, create similar patterns. You are creating the ripple effect of Love going viral, touching everyone and everything.

Finally, you are beginning to realize how powerful you are as Love expresses life through and as you. We are not referring to ego's use of the word powerful, but the soul's interpretation which is a force for good, a demonstration of God's presence as Love. Just as you have had an impact and influence on plants, animals, and others, you now begin to see that the power of Love can be an instrument you bring to situations, circumstances, events, and other areas where extreme confusion, agitation, and inharmonious energies are present. You learn that the Love you are has the power to dissolve all that is not real. The beauty of this is that you never need to put yourself in harm's way again. It would be impossible at this stage. You have the power to direct your consciousness of Love wherever it is needed most.

Do you realize yet and fully accept what you truly are? You are amazing and infinitely spectacular. I hope you see that. I pray that you will allow this love to shine brightly and touch everyone you meet or even think of. As you awaken and examine these ten symptoms of enlightenment, more and more will be revealed to you.

Before we move to the third symptom of enlightenment, I'd like to share a beautiful and simple little story that demonstrates the influence of Love's presence. A dear friend of mine tells how his wife, at Christmas time not too long ago, won a poinsettia plant at a holiday business event. She brought it home and set it on a table near their sliding glass door where it would receive partial sun as well as shade.

It was a pathetic-looking gift with two branches and about three leaves, two of which were just about ready to fall off, with the third barely clinging to life. The new surroundings didn't seem to help much and neither did the fresh water. As they began to consider moving the plant out, thinking its days were over, my friend suggested they try a little experiment so they could attempt to prove, model, and demonstrate the power of Love as described in this chapter.

The plant was moved to a table near a kitchen window where it would receive about the same amount of sun and shade as in its former spot, but it would intentionally receive much more attention. It sat where it would be noticed every morning when the couple would start their day. The gentleman went out of his way to speak to the plant and tell her how beautiful she was. He thanked her all day every day for the beauty she displayed and the gift of life she is.

On and on this went. This little poinsettia received love and praise day in and day out. It didn't take long for this fragile life to respond. It seemed that every day a new leaf was being born. It now has well over one hundred leaves as it moves into the summer months over six months removed from the Christmas holiday. The man was heartbroken one day as he accidentally pulled off two leaves and the little virgin branch they were clinging to. He spoke to the leaves and apologized. He said "I love you" over and over and placed the leaves in some water. He was amazed when they remained vibrant as if they heard his plea to keep on living. One day he simply removed the two leaves and their stem and placed them back in the dirt next to their source. Those two leaves have turned into four and a whole new plant has been born.

Born out of Love, just like YOU!

Symptom #3:

Depth of Interaction

Every encounter you have with another, no matter how mundane, feels holy and blessed.

The difference between ego's perspective on life and the soul's is like the difference between a shallow pond and the depths of an ocean. Every other concept has fallen away and yet something new has been released: a profound longing to love everyone in every moment, no matter what. This automatically brings great depth to every conversation, every interaction, and every movement. Every encounter you have with another person, no matter how normal it may seem, feels Divine. And the ability to return to shallow interactions completely disappears. It doesn't matter if you are with a saint or sinner, you are suddenly able to look through all of those seeming differences to the truth within, the holy ONE at the center of everyone you meet.

This experience is enough to lift you above those former interactions. You find yourself wondering how you could have held such shallow spaces before. If someone tries to interact with you on that level, you smile and gently move on. There is no judgment, just an inability to see anything other than the light that shines through every interaction.

And that is the key. The ability to perceive that the shadow in yourself or anyone else has left. All you see is the light, and its radiance transcends the world. You realize that you are not interacting with human beings at all, but with the soul of each person you encounter. Though this is only the third symptom of enlightenment, it is one of the most profound and meaningful. This is where the difference between the world you once perceived and this new vision becomes most clear. It is an experience you cannot explain, except to say to each person you meet, either silently or aloud:

"I love you more than you could ever
begin to imagine.'

You are beginning to understand that you are what Love is. You are beginning to grasp how ubiquitous the infinite Love you are is. This awakening is like a staircase. The previous step brought the realization of what you are, your awakening to the Love that is your very essence. Now you move beyond just being what Love is into a deeper engagement with life and living. It could be said that this is the *action* or *doing* aspect of the Love you are. However, you would have to consider the paradox involved here. The action is not really an activity other than seeing truth, feeling deeply, loving unconditionally, and being in a state of non-judgment. So, the action, the doing, is found within being! This will be explored as you move forward and, in even more depth, enter symptom number four.

What is important for you to understand is that Divine Love is found through living everything. One Source. One Reality. One Presence. One Power. One Love.

Let us circle back for a moment to bring more clarity and meaning to this step on your staircase of enlightenment. Have you slowed down enough to realize that where you are right now, in this eternal moment of here and now, you are standing on Holy Ground? Wherever you are God is. There is no place you can go and no place you could ever be where God is not. You are made of God. You are

One with God. You are God pressing out into visibility to experience life as you. You have come to know that God is Love and Love is God. So, you can now make this same statement interchanging God and Love. Here it is: wherever you are Love is. There is no place you can ever go and no place you could ever be where Love is not. You are made of Love. You are one with Love. You have at last come to know that Love is God and God is Love.

This might be a good time to call to mind the affirmation I gave you previously:

"The holy sacred presence of Love is wholly present in me and as me. I Am the holy, sacred Presence of Love. I Am that, I Am."

Continue to affirm this, writing these words on your heart. Continue to say this out loud until you feel the truth and reality of this statement. Go back and forth interchanging the word God and Love.

"The holy sacred presence of God is wholly present in me and as me. I Am the holy, sacred Presence of God. I Am that, I Am."

Breathe. Let the Truth of these affirmative statements wash over your soul and penetrate all that you are.

Let us look more closely at how this applies to your path to enlightenment. This affirmation of Truth, this statement that feels so good affirming, knowing, understanding, and being, is also true for everyone else! Indeed, you are the holy, sacred, Presence of the Divine, so you are always standing on Holy Ground and so is everyone you encounter.

If you fully accept this symptom as an essential part of your awakening and the Truth you are coming to know, you will understand that it can be no other way. From this knowing perspective, every encounter you have with another will be felt deep within your soul. You will sense the sacredness of all who cross your holy path. It matters not where they might be on their path of unfoldment. All that matters is your knowing.

Being non-judgmental is the key here. At this stage of your awakening the tendency to judge, which has perhaps been a big part of your human experience, begins to fade away. Your soul sees only what is real and that is Love. By its very nature, Divine Love is unconditional and since this is the actual substance from which you were made, you are waking up to your essence, the essence that understands what the word unconditional means. No conditions. There is nothing you must do to fully realize that you are made of Divine Substance. Love is inherent in all that is, and Love is the very essence of Life. This is the Holy One at the center of everyone you meet.

You may be wondering where all those dark shadows have disappeared to. Where are the uncomfortable differences you often felt when you were asleep groping around in the dark? Don't look for them. They are not here. All that is not real and all that is not true has dissolved in the Light of Love that now illumines your pathway. Keep moving along your way being Love and greeting the Love you meet by loving deeply and unconditionally.

At this frequency words are often unspoken. You realize that everyone may not be at the same place on the path where your light is now shining. You simply accept everyone as they are knowing that the awakening will come for each one of them at the right time, in the right way, in the right place as they all move along this path of Light.

Not everyone is looking at the same sheet of music at the same time, but this doesn't mean they will not eventually join in the same song. Stick to the melody even if you are the only one listening and continue singing your song of Love.

I love taking in all the beauty nature provides, whether it is standing on the beach looking at the Gulf of Mexico, seeing the immensity of the Pacific Ocean from an elevated plateau, or standing at the foot of a magnificent mountain range. When I bear witness to such beauty I always give thanks for the majesty of creation and the givingness of God. I stand in awe at the plethora of ways God expresses the Love that God IS through beauty and grace. This is truly what being Love is.

At this stage of your enlightenment, you realize you are both the giver and the gift, the lover and the beloved, the creator and the created. Look to nature and the *givingness* of God as a bouquet of love that is ceaselessly being handed to you through grace. Always remember: God is God and God is Love. This alone will suffice.

And, of course, this is what you are as well. You are now seeing with the eyes of grace. You are moving into the realization that there are no others. I like to call this the God's-eye view. The idea or concept of otherness has passed away, replaced by a vision of holiness so bright that every illusion dissolves on its own.

I invite you to call on your imagination for a moment. See yourself boarding a spaceship designed for tourists. You get settled in and you are very excited about the journey that is about to take place. There are very large windows all around the craft. There is not a bad seat anywhere. Everyone can see everything. You are buckled in, you are comfortable, you are secure and you are thrilled to have been selected for this experience. It is time for lift-off.

Looking out the windows you can see friends, family, and even strangers waving at you and your traveling companions. The countdown begins, then lift-off. Moving away from the launch pad at a very high rate of speed, it is only a matter of seconds before the friends, family, and strangers you were just waving at blend into one. There is no way to distinguish one from the other but you are still waving at the whole group. Very quickly you experience a bird's eye view as you find yourself soaring above houses and buildings. Cars look like toys and anything smaller begins to dissolve as the distance increases.

As you move through a thin layer of clouds you realize how quickly you have risen above everything in the physical world. In this moment you see only lush greenery, bodies of water, and perhaps the illusion of lines that separate one farmer's crop and field from another. Rising higher you find the clouds you just moved through are all below you now but they are very thin and spread out so you can still see the earth. Higher and higher you soar. At last, you have reached the intended orbit that will be maintained for the duration of your trip.

Imagine how you would feel, especially if this is something you have wanted to do your entire life. You would likely be feeling tremendous joy, elation, and love for this spectacular moment. A sense of tremendous awe would be washing over you as you take in the magnificence of God's creation. One giant ball of color and light floating in space below you. Breathe. Receive the gift right here and right now. You have finally reached God's view of the world.

Now I invite you to look at this experience through the lens of Love, observing everything from an ethereal perspective. Consider these questions as you observe yourself, your thoughts, and your feelings as you experience this great awakening:

When you were making your way to the spaceship with your fellow travelers, were you thinking about how different you are or whether they might irritate or annoy you?

Of course not. You were completely engrossed in the moment filled with anticipation, and so were the others. So much so that it didn't feel like there were any others. You were together, you were one, you were united as you walked. You felt only Love.

When you were buckled in, secure and comfortable did you fall asleep or did you feel the excitement building and a great feeling of love for everyone on board?

All you felt was Love, and it was the same for each one of them. You all knew Love was real as you shared and exuded pure joy.

When you waved to friends and strangers looking out the window, were you thinking about how different they all are?

No, you were receiving their loving wishes and the joy they felt for you. You felt your mutual bond in the eternal moment of living love.

As you moved up, up, and away, did you notice how the group of people below blended into One? Did you notice how differences not only didn't matter, but they also didn't even make sense anymore?

The only thing that mattered was the variety of God expressing Love in so many different ways, pressing out as Love.

Once you reached your orbit did you see everything as One, as God would perceive it, born of Love and given as a gift from your Source?

From this God's eye view, nothing and no one is left out. There is only Love and Love expressing.

From this perspective, it is so much easier to see and feel and know that only Love is real.

I invite you to continue to move through this imagined experience over and over again and relate it to your journey on your path of awakening. Use this as an exercise to help you see everything and everyone through the eyes of God, which is through the eyes of unending Love.

There are no others, only variations of Love expressing Itself. Every encounter, every interaction, every conversation, every act of loving kindness, every thought, word, and action is Divine, sacred, and blessed, for we recognize that we are all standing on Holy Ground wherever we may be.

At this stage, we know and feel that only Love is real.

Symptom #4:

A Sense of Inaction

The need to DO anything has been replaced by the desire to BE everything.

Have you ever experienced a time when you felt a great need or responsibility to be successful in life? Most of us were raised with the idea that doing important things should make us happy and successful. And even if you are successful in some area of your life, does that automatically lead to happiness and contentment?

The fourth symptom of enlightenment is feeling that you have been released from the need to DO and have increased your desire to simply BE. Some may interpret this as laziness or inaction, and at first, it may seem to be exactly that. It begins with the need to hold still, to rest in the knowledge that your holiness is not based on what you produce but on the inherent value of your soul. The statement "I need do nothing" resonates deeply with the soul, while ego interprets it as the supreme insult.

Most people spend their lives rushing around engaged in constant, strenuous activity, believing that if they just keep moving, they will not have to deal with the deeper pulse of the soul. This still, quiet voice can only be heard when you hold still and listen deeply. The need to DO interrupts this flow. It distracts us, and we willingly accept this distraction. Why? Because a part of us, our ego, is afraid of what it will mean. It is afraid that you will turn control of your life over to your soul and it will lose the power it has claimed until now. It wants you to keep moving, to keep striving, and to keep the wheel spinning. Releasing the need to DO is the greatest threat to its supposed power.

You may feel that the activities and pursuits of the past are no longer in alignment with your new life. When I was younger, I was an excellent salesman, then when I went through the initial stages of my awakening, I found it difficult, almost impossible to sell anything. The drive a salesman must have to be successful simply disappeared. I didn't care about making huge amounts of money and it no longer mattered if I was at the top of my field. The only thing that mattered was following that inner voice and allowing it to lead the way into this new life I felt breaking through the soil of my consciousness. There were many days when I would find an open church and simply sit for hours without doing anything. It didn't take long for my manager to realize I was completely unproductive, bringing an abrupt end to that stage of my career.

But one thing that never dissipated was my desire to create, especially writing music. The more I stepped back and listened to that still, quiet voice, the more productive I was in my creative endeavors. I liken this to a musical instrument, perhaps a guitar. A guitar does not play itself. The strings do not begin to vibrate until the musician picks up the instrument and begins to strum. Then music fills the air. It reminds us that we are all called to relax in the arms of the master musician and not try to do anything on our own, but simply BE an instrument of peace.

Peace, be still. Just sit with these words for a moment: peace, be, being, still, stillness, tranquility, serenity. Words have energy and if you would slow down enough to spend some time with these words and others that I will share later, you may feel a silent harmony that resonates with your Soul. Take some time and be with these words right now.

Notice I didn't say do something with these words, I just instructed you to be with them. What I want most to communicate is that the doing is in the being. For now, just remember that.

In a way, I did ask you to do something but what I asked you to do was just be. Can you see this distinction? Welcome to the concept of *"be, do, have"* which we will explore in this section.

I look at this fourth symptom of enlightenment as another one of the beautiful stages in this experience of awakening. Especially when the light bulb goes off and you really and truly get it as a deep, profound understanding.

The doing is in the being.

Let those words echo throughout your soul. Let those words echo throughout your entire being.

Now notice the doing part of that last statement. You are letting which means you are allowing.

I don't want to rush through this with you. I want you to continue to feel your way into this. Most likely you are already experiencing this symptom, however, it may seem very strange to you in the beginning without understanding exactly what

66

is happening, so I intend to hold your hand and lead you into a place of clarity.

What am I doing? I am being a guide, serving, being Love.

"The doing is in the being."

Let us dive deeper into this experience. Be with these words for at least several minutes. They are found in Psalm 46:10:

"Be still and know that I Am God"

Repeat this verse several times softly and slowly, again feeling, reaching into the harmony that resonates with your Soul.

Moving out of your intellect and into your Soul, let this phrase sink even deeper as you watch it reduce, word by word, into one of the most powerful expressions from any sacred scripture:

Be still and know that I Am God.

Be still and know that I Am.

Be still and know that I.

Be still and know that.

Be still and know.

Be still.

Be.

I suggest you be with this for several minutes, breathing your way through it many times. How do you feel now as you drink this in as if it is a fine glass of wine? Do you feel lighter? Do you feel as if a door has opened inside you? Remember:

"The doing is in the being."

You are probably feeling a sense of calm and peacefulness settling into your whole self right now. You are touching serenity, inner harmony, and tranquility. This is the concept of *"be, do, have"* illustrated in a very simple way. Through understanding, you can apply this to your path of enlightenment. You no longer *"do, do, do"* to simply get and acquire goods. You are learning to *be* that which you are. You are seeing that sacred doing is in the being and therefore what you are being you will have, which will always be the will of God for your Life and the purpose of your Soul.

Let's stay with this a little while longer, exchanging the word God with the word Love.

"Be still and know that I Am Love."

Remember, I AM is the holy sacred name of God and it is also what you are at the level of Soul. I

Am is your Truth. I Am is the Real you. I Am is God. I Am is Love. I often use the words Christ Consciousness and Soul interchangeably. These terms refer to the Truth of your being as opposed to ego. Also, ego is sometimes referred to as personality or identity.

As you move through the fourth symptom of enlightenment, ego often remains contentious. Ego wants to always win and be the dominant player in this ongoing battle. Please understand I AM not saying that ego and personality are bad and that they should be done away with all together. They are the condiments that, in the right proportion, give your Soul the delightful flavor as you move through life. What is yours to do is simply to recognize what you are being in any given moment by asking whether it is coming from Love or ego's power play. Being Love keeps ego playing second fiddle which is, of course, its rightful place.

With this awareness, I invite you to go back to the verse we have been working with and this time, feel it speaking directly to ego, perhaps even affirming the phrase while looking in the mirror.

Be still (ego) and know that I Am (Soul) God.

Be still (ego) and know that I AM Love (my Real and True essence).

This is a beautiful exercise to work with as you move through all of these symptoms of enlightenment.

Be still and know that I Am Love.

Be still and know that I Am.

Be still and know that I, (I as in the Individuality I Am, Soul).

Be still and know that (ego, don't forget that!).

Be still and know.

Be still.

Be.

It all comes down to Being.

"The doing is in the being."

When your will becomes focused on being, it will naturally move you into the natural flow of what is yours to do. What is yours to do is that which brings you into alignment with your Soul's purpose. AS Love expressing, you have been endowed with certain gifts that are meant to be shared. This is your Light and it is yours to shine.

When you do this, you are being authentically you and you will attract everything that supports this in ways you can not even imagine.

Can you see now how ego and personality get confused as they ceaselessly pursue activity? They mistakenly believe that activity equals productivity and so they are in a constant state of pursuing something the Soul isn't even interested in. This is the reason why most people who are asleep to the Truth of their Being always feel an inner longing and discontentment with nearly everything. Satisfaction will only come when you are being the Love you are and expressing that Love by shining your Light.

When you release the need to always be doing something, you will find more time to enter the silence. Being in the silence and being aware of the Presence of God within you, answers will come, and directions and guidance will come. This is the secret place of the Most-High and it is where you will find the greatest rest.

What you previously felt as laziness and a call to inaction are the inner promptings of Spirit calling you home. Pay attention, which means be attentive. I wrote earlier about words and the energy they carry. Look at the words *inspiration* and *intuition*. Both start with the word In, and that should tell you something important. Inspiration is to be 'in' spirit receiving divine influence. Intuition is spiritual insight; divine communication and wisdom downloaded from Infinite Intelligence.

"The doing is in the being."

"Be still and listen."

I listened in the silence to that still small voice guiding me to be creative, to share music and song, and to be a light of peace in this world. Likewise, at this stage, you are being guided to listen, too. You are waking up and it is being noticed. Your Inner Spirit is saying: "Slow down. Spend some time inside. I have some directions for you."

This is your call to be transformed by the renewing of your mind, to quote our friend Paul from Romans 12:2:

"Do not conform to the pattern of this world, but be transformed by the renewing of your mind. Then you will be able to test and approve what God's will is—his good, pleasing and perfect will."

Transformation — transitioning from living life dominated by ego and worldly pursuits to living inspired. Being transformed takes place when you allow your mind, through your thoughts, to be renewed. This is to make new, to be restored, rolling everything back to the purity and pristine state of being unconditioned by ego's influence and desires. From this renewed state you begin to clearly hear the voice of your Soul.

You can make the comparison to our personal computers and smartphones. They are getting faster and faster and are able to do more and more. Most of the time they are doing so many things at once that it is incomprehensible. If you have ever spent time sharing your screen with a technical wizard trying to troubleshoot your computer, you know what I mean. They will often open our task manager to have a look at all the programs running in the background. There are hundreds of them and if you are like me you probably don't know what any of them are doing.

Very often the technical wizard will say it is just trying to do too much. You may have complicated the situation more by doing things, clicking things, and opening even more things thinking this might solve your problem. It doesn't take long for you to discover that this *doing* is not the answer. The device becomes more bogged down and performs slower and slower because it is trying to do too much. Sometimes it shuts down and stops running completely.

The technician notices all the *doing* that has been going on and after exhaustive efforts finally knows that the only solution is to stop doing so many things. You are told to shut down the computer, unplug it and just let it be. After this period of allowing the computer to be refreshed, you try a restart. If it starts up it usually doesn't take long before habit takes over and you start doing too much again and receive the same results.

This time the techno wiz tells you you have gone too far. It is time for a system renewal. You are told that the operating system and the memory have to be restored to their original uncorrupted condition.

In other words, it has to be transformed by the renewing of its mind!

And so it is with you as you come to experience this fourth symptom of enlightenment. Thank goodness you are awakening at just the right time. You have noticed these things and you have taken a deep dive into learning more about your condition. You get to keep what has served you well along your way as wisdom is gained and you can make the conscious choice to leave out all the rest. You see through the lens of Love the many disguises ego wears in its attempt to make you think you are going the wrong way. Now you know that you don't have to keep moving every moment of every day. Now you know that it is time to stop rushing. Now you know that there is no need and no point in *doing, doing, doing* all the time without giving any consideration to what you are *being*.

Within this fourth symptom of enlightenment, you now know that you have finally been released from the need to DO and have amplified your desire to simply BE.

In other words, you have discovered:

"The doing is in the being."

Be still and know that you are Love.

Be still and know that you are.

Be still and know that You.

Be still and know that.

Be still and know.

Be still.

Be.

Simply Be...

"The doing is in the being."

Symptom #5:

A Feeling of Timelessness

Time loses its meaning and importance; only the present moment matters.

Timelessness is the great undoing of ego which relies upon time to assert its control and to fulfill its ultimate goal — your death. This may sound strange but when you look at the inevitability of bodily death and ego's need for you to completely identify with the body, time becomes its ally. Time, after all, offers a beginning and an end to everything you experience. As long as you are bound by the rules of time, ego feels happy and secure.

The truth within is not a body. Remember, you are the truth that is forever true, and this truth is not bound by time or space. Therefore, as you go through the early stages of your awakening you identify more with the infinite world than the finite perspective you have claimed until now. As you begin to experience your infinite nature, the need to follow the rules of time begins to fade. You are no longer afraid of what might happen to the body

77

because you KNOW that it could never encompass the truth within you. This knowledge is the essence of what it means to be awake.

Your body is a vehicle of communication and the means through which you move through the world. It is like a car that you use to go to the store or go on a cross-country journey. But you have probably never thought that you are synonymous with your car. At the same time, it is important for you to take care of your vehicle. You change the oil and take it to the repair shop if anything breaks. The same applies to the body. The fact that you are no longer bound by time, or that you have at least begun the process of releasing this need, does not mean that you should abuse the body. It is a gift that is meant to be cared for, but when the gift is no longer needed, it is laid aside. Yes, there will come a point at which the body no longer fulfills its function, but the truth of you is eternal, and the experience of this infinite nature is becoming your single focus.

The present moment offers you everything you want. This is the timeless instant of your release from ego's attempt to control your destiny. Your destiny has already been fulfilled, and this is the last thing ego wants you to recognize. It puts your destiny far into the distance and claims that you have much work to do before you arrive at your goal. But the ultimate goal of life is to realize that you are *not* your body and your soul is eternal and there is nothing the soul could ever need that is not already contained within its eternal space. The only thing you need is to realize that time cannot claim the holy, perfect extension of love that you are and have always been. Every limitation falls away in this bright light and is replaced by the reality you have pushed away until now. But now the light is too bright to deny. You are awake and no shadow can claim you.

Once this is fully realized, you will feel as if the chains have finally been broken. You have turned the corner and your Soul shouts for joy, proclaiming liberty at last while ego cries liberty has been lost. Your Soul has always been aware of its own divinity and you are waking up to this immortal Reality. Now you must notice when your attention drifts, then discern if it is ego pulling you away from your awareness of the present moment. Always notice what you are noticing.

Speaking of noticing, have you noticed how these symptoms or steps build on each other and work together? When it comes to noticing what you are noticing, you are really drawing on what we have explored in a previous section. Specifically, you will want to notice not only *what* you are being in any given moment, but also *where* you are being. Where is your awareness right now? Is your awareness in this eternal present moment of right now? Ask: am I being fully present right here and right now as the holy sacred presence of God I Am?

Meditation and mindfulness will help you strengthen this present moment awareness muscle. Mindfulness invites you to be fully present now, without judgment. When you learn to practice mindfulness meditation, you are instructed to pay attention to your awareness, always gently guiding it back to this present moment should it start to drift in other directions. This is so important at this stage of your awakening, to learn that you are always in control of your awareness, and you have the ability to move it to wherever you will it to be.

To illustrate this, close your eyes while comfortably sitting in a chair, placing your palms up as your hands rest on your thighs or knees. Take a few deep breaths just to help you relax and anchor into this moment. Now place your full awareness in the palm of your right hand and just leave it there for a few moments. Then move your awareness to your left palm and hold it there for a few moments. Notice what you are noticing. Did you notice how easy it was to do this? Did you feel your awareness sitting there in your right hand and then your left? This was a simple example, but you can do this, moving your awareness all over your physical body, then even outside your body. You can experiment with this during your time in meditation and throughout your day as you practice being mindful in this eternal moment of now.

This isn't a book about mindfulness meditation but it is important for you to know that you are in control of your awareness. Practice and always notice what you are noticing. Is your attention drifting to days gone by and events that have already taken place? Is your awareness remaining centered on the holy, sacred presence of God you are? When it is, you will have more and more of the experience of timelessness, if you aren't already. This is entering the Kingdom of Heaven and there are no clocks there.

Have you noticed that if you allow yourself to spend too much time looking at your life through the rear-view mirror you are much more likely to sink into a depressed emotional state? Likewise, if you spend too much time focusing on a future point that doesn't exist, you are more likely to be filled with anxiety, extreme apprehension and even dreading a tomorrow that isn't real in this moment. Always notice what you are noticing, then course-correct, if necessary, without judgment. Your desire to remain fully awake is all that matters.

We read in Genesis "Let there be Light." In this story of creation, it doesn't say let there be light for a little while and then shut it off again after an hour or two, or in three days or six months – then bring back the darkness. No, it says "Let there be Light." Always, with no end, let it continue and be infinite and eternal. And so it is with your enlightenment. Once you move into the Light that awakens, you will clearly see that you are not your body, and you have no beginning and no end.

This symptom of enlightenment isn't about death and dying. It is about life and living. Let us go back to your awareness of what you are. You are the holy sacred presence of God, the holy sacred presence of Love, Right Now. There was never a point in time when you were not this Presence that has always been Present. There may be a point in time when you noticed this Light within you and when you did, it was a moment you were fully aware of. You noticed something that has always been present. You didn't wake up one day and come to believe it was right around the corner, marking a future date on your calendar when you expected to meet up with it. Neither did you realize enlightenment a long time ago, only to see it vanish. In either case, it was you and your awareness that was not fully present in the eternal moment of right now. It is in this moment that you find God and your own infinite eternal nature. It is in this moment where God lives pressing out into visibility as the Love you are and all that is real and immortal. It is here that time loses its meaning and importance, and ego's death grip weakens, losing all of its strength and power. All you have ever really wanted is right here and freedom tastes good.

I mentioned the story of creation earlier and I'd like you to engage your imagination to go deeper into this story. There are two things to notice from an eternal, infinite perspective. You are most likely already experiencing this fifth symptom. This doesn't mean that your ego will not continue making attempts to infiltrate your state of enlightenment.

Consider: All there is from God's perspective strengthens the barricade that rises to prevent penetration from ego's cunning ways. Putting your imagination to use in your awakened state will also help you to move out of your intellect and into a place of spaciousness where your mind can more easily consider the illogical. Ego will no longer be able to tolerate that which lies beyond human comprehension and will try to persuade you to not even try.

My friend, the late Dr. Wayne W. Dyer, would often ask his readers to consider that moment in time just before they were conceived and their humanness began to take form. So, I will ask you here: Where were you? *Something* cannot come from *nothing*. Using your imagination, contemplate where you were, what it was like, and what were you being in that moment. I want to reiterate that you are not your body. Your body is simply a temporary garment of your Soul. As you imagine this, you will most likely sense a state of unity and oneness with all there is. Yet you made the choice to press out into visibility, to experience humanity as the self you are now. On this path of enlightenment, or remembering your Divinity, you are now awakening to the *how* of expression. Knowing this, the realization of timelessness takes hold. It also becomes apparent that the *how* is to simply be what Love is in all ways and always. And the place where this is accomplished is the eternal moment of right here and right now.

God ceaselessly presses out as Life and Love to experience more Life and Love in an infinite number of ways. Look around you right now. Even from your limited human perspective you can see and experience the abundance of Life expressing Life. Now, knowing that God is Love and Love is God, would not the *givingness* that God exudes extend to your Soul, which is who you really are? In other words, would your Soul not have boundless opportunities to be Life, experience Life, and live Life in an infinite variety of ways? For now, just hold that thought.

Stay here with me for a moment longer as we continue to imagine the infinite scale of NOW. Everyone who knows me knows that I'm a big Star

Wars fan, so you can imagine my excitement as I contemplated something that was recently presented to us by scientists and astronomers. Astronomers had been noticing an area in the universe that seemed to be completely void of light. Nothing was visible in this area, no stars, no planets, not even a trace of light. A total massive area of nothing but darkness. Was this the edge of space? Was this a black hole so massive that its outer fringe was beyond anything that could be observed by human means? Was this the point where the universe left off and nothingness began? These questions and others greatly puzzled scientists and astronomers.

They decided to point the Hubble space telescope at this massive dark area and left it there for eleven days. The data that came back was absolutely mind-boggling! The telescope picked up light sources coming from billions and billions of stars and galaxies, and planets determined to be thirteen billion light years away, that is 880 sextillion miles! Until that moment the scientists believed they were looking at an infinite void when, in reality, they were observing infinite LIFE.

Here is my point. Would God — as your Creator and Source — have created such a vast

Universe and at the same time, created this thing we call time without giving you the capacity to experience every bit of it? Would God — as your Source, being the Creator of all that is and being the very essence of Love — press out into the Universe as your Soul, but only in a limited way? That would be absurd because God, abiding by Its own infinite Beingness, would not be able to do that. There is no limitation in God other than the illusion of limitation.

This being the case, consider that you — the Real You, the holy, sacred You, your Soul — being one with God, have not only been gifted with eternal life but are in fact experiencing it right now. Since time is the measure of something from its beginning to its end and since life is infinite, it would only make sense that, in Absolute Reality, time doesn't even exist. Your Soul is free to forever live as Love — God expressing, radiating the Love you are made of — in every nook and cranny of this infinite Universe if you choose to do so. It all starts with your awakening into your timeless beingness.

The un-illumined intellect continues to identify with the human body and ceaselessly asks 'what time is it?' Your ego lives here too, looking at the clock. Remember, it is always working to draw you into an emotional state of either sadness, by reminding you of days gone by that will never be again, or by creating worry about a future point in time that doesn't exist. You know better now. You are infinite and eternal Love. You now realize that eternal Life isn't something that begins when you die, it is something that has always been, and you live there now.

If you are comfortable with all the side effects contained within this symptom, congratulations. You have made it home to the place where you now recognize you will always be Love.

Symptom #6:

Attachment to Special

Relationships Has Diminished

Every person you meet is the Beloved in disguise, replacing the desire to elevate certain relationships over others.

It is at this stage of the awakening that many people abandon ship and revert back to a life where special relationships are of primary importance. They have yet to grasp an essential part of whole-mindedness: that nothing can be lost when you embrace everything. Read that last sentence again because it is of critical importance at this stage: nothing can be lost when you embrace everything simply because everyone you love is contained within everything.

Ego-mind is completely incapable of understanding the simplicity of this statement. It believes that everything is uncountable, but the soul recognizes that everything is really only ONE thing. As always, this is not something that can be understood by the intellectual mind but is perfectly understandable and clear to your soul or your Whole-Mind.

Let us examine this for another moment. The purpose of a special relationship is to carve out a private space where love and devotion can be shared with one person, or a small group of people, at the exclusion of everyone else. Exclusion is its goal, not inclusion. Inclusion is an attribute of the soul and is completely foreign to ego. Ego believes that you lose what you love when you embrace everything. This thought is clearly insane but is accepted as true until you come to the beginning stages of the awakening you are experiencing now.

This is when you realize that everything you love is contained within everything you love. Does that make sense? Of course, it doesn't, and that is the point. But you may feel something beginning to move inside you when you hear these words, just as a mother feels her unborn child moving within her before it is finally born. You are waking up, and the truth within you is beginning to fill in all those empty spaces that have been ignored until now.

You are like the woman who has come full term. There is no stopping the birth and the love you feel for the child that is about to be born has no earthly comparison. The unborn child moves within you because it knows that its time has come; the moment of its birth into a new world. You are both the mother and the child being born. It is the experience of your wholeness that is about to be birthed. Just relax and allow the experience of this new life to overtake you.

Love is One, that is all you need to know for now. When this ripens within you, you will discover a deep care and love for everyone, including those who are closest to you.

Give yourself some time with this one. Resist the urge to go back to sleep. You don't have to make yourself do anything here. In fact, at this stage of your awakening, you couldn't force anything even if you tried. Enlightenment isn't like that. It unfolds and moves in as you allow it to. You wake up and you begin to see things, especially others, in a different way and in a different light. You see others as they truly are, what they truly are and from what you truly are, unconditional Love. Here you are coming to know what I meant when I wrote, "you will begin to realize that there are no others."

Let us look at unconditional Love again, specifically, the meaning of the word unconditional. At this stage, you — as unconditional Love expressing itself — have abandoned the selection process you previously spent so much time expressing. This selection process has been going on throughout your life both consciously and unconsciously from the very beginning. At this stage of your spiritual growth, you are no longer focused on who's in and who's out. Unconditional Love is unconditional; no conditions. Period. And remember, Unconditional Love is what you are: your very essence. Therefore, the former selection process and standards for admittance to your inner circle have been left on ego's doorstep.

Since Absolute Love has no conditions and no requirements, you have finally recognized that any bias, conscious or unconscious, needs to be identified and released. At this stage, a selection process based on anything other than being what unconditional Love *is* is useless to you. If you allow your ego to cling to this routine, you will notice how it weighs you down and becomes burdensome, even preventing you from rising into the higher levels of consciousness.

Don't beat yourself up if this doesn't come in an instant. It will come as you make the choice to live into Love. Ego wants to be in charge, ego thrives on contests and competition and raises the gate to admit anyone who successfully wins by sufficiently puffing it up. Ego will reject anyone who is a perceived threat to its pedestal and its favorite weapon is seeing to it that love is withheld. Ego requires the spotlight and a chorus of:

"me, me, me, me, me!"

Ego seeks adulation, and the pride and recognition it desires are mistaken for love.

Be Love. See Love. Drop out of your head and into your heart. Get comfortable with the illogical. Mind your mind. This is how you get your Divine Self to join the team.

One of the reasons this may seem difficult to comprehend is because ego reads only certain words that make it through the me-me filter. It is as if ego is looking through a keyhole believing it sees the whole picture. With limited information, it sees this stage of enlightenment and the words I used to begin this chapter as the ultimate threat. To ego, it feels like this is about releasing all special relationships and pushing the love you experience in those relationships to the side or even abandoning them altogether. Not only is this not true, but in actuality, quite the opposite is unfolding.

You are making the transition into soul-based living. The foundation for all your thoughts, words, actions, and emotional state, along with anything and everything in between, is unconditional love. In other words, you now live the Truth you are. It is not that what you have previously called elevated special relationships are done away with, but that *everything* is now elevated. From here you see All through the lens of unconditional Love and therefore wrapped and weaved into your life experience as more Love, more God expressing, as everyone and everything. Ego spends a great deal of time searching to see blemishes in others as well as the personality characteristics and behaviors that are either not good enough in ego's eyes or are too aggressive and therefore a danger to ego's throne.

If you are still trying to wrap your head around this, it means ego is still in charge and you haven't moved from your head to your heart, then deeper into your soul. The key here is willingness.

You can't just say, "Well, I want to be fully awakened and experience enlightenment so I'll just do this, just fake it.". That is not the way it works. However, if you are at least *willing* to drop any and all conditions, if you are *willing* to see everyone from on high, as they truly are, one with God, you will begin the process of swinging the gate wide open. Soon you will know that nothing can be lost when you embrace everything. The old way of ego will seem absurd. You will feel your way into this stage more than anything else because you will finally know, really know, that everyone you love is contained within everything.

Although each of these stages of enlightenment is really an awakening into full awareness of the Truth of your Being, your essence, which is Love, there are exercises and practices you can engage in to assist you along your way. You should have noticed by now that each symptom you experience is really a breakthrough to a higher expression of the same experience. As always, it is the experience of enlightenment that counts, not the intellectual concepts.

At this stage of your awakening, you are beginning to realize or have a full experience of the fact that Love is the only true reality. Each day you should set the intention to live fully from your love essence.

My dear friend and colleague Martha Creek, in her book <u>Martha's Pearls: A Spiritual Approach to Life</u>, shares a simple exercise that should really help you with this stage. I share it here with her permission:

> "We are given so many opportunities to live with intention, fully awake to each other and to our broader/enlarged selves in the world. What opportunity will you radically seize to break through old ways of being and create anew?

> "If you haven't begun yet, it's not too late. Let's take a little journey together. Close your eyes and reach out your hand and heart to your loved ones. One by one, gather each of them into your heart space. Be sure to get those who have harmed you or who are estranged. We are being radical remember? Connect with them. Now, extend that expanded warmth and love out to someone you don't know, that perhaps you meet at the

bank, gas station, or grocery store. Once you have connected with them, call to mind someone in another state or country that you know and connect your heart light with them. Hold them in your heart and surround each with your best blessing.

"Now, extend this out across the globe. Literally hold in mind someone in another country and even an entire country: kids at play, workers in a field, all races, all religions, social status, everyone. Wherever they are, hold them in your mind and heart with love. Do you see them? You are deeply connected with them. Offer this web of love from your highest consciousness. Bless each soul and their journey.

"Receive as you have given. This creating is free, and one radical way to give to yourself, to others, and to the world. Gift yourself and the world in thoughts and actions."

I love this exercise and I really encourage you to practice it on a regular basis. Feel free to be creative as you put it into your daily routine. Visualize the gates swinging open and everyone joining you in the place of Love you call home. See yourself moving through the world physically, mentally, emotionally, and spiritually, in every thought, word and action, being a beacon of loving light welcoming everyone home. Remember there is no gatekeeper here. If you find that your ego is becoming a pest, simply give it something to do. It may even feel included and finally begin playing the role it was meant to play: becoming the servant of the soul.

If you are consistent in the daily effort of utilizing this visualization tool and other tools like this, your life will begin resembling that which you have pictured in your mind. Before you know it, you will be looking for ways to include and accept everyone rather than searching for and finding reasons why they should be excluded. This will be a natural unfolding in your awakening process as you continue to flower and bloom.

Before you move along to explore symptom number seven let us have a brief review of the necessary elements you need to understand at this stage in your progress.

Unconditional Love

This is the Absolute and the Absolute is perfect, whole, pure, complete, and without conditions. Absolute Unconditional Love is without restrictions of any kind because it is incapable of expressing anything opposed to its experience. This is the infinite and eternal All. This is infinite and eternal Reality and Truth. This is also your Source, what you are made of and therefore what you are in Reality.

Accepting, Allowing and Inclusive

Living from your essence of Love, you now know that everything and everyone is included here. Nothing is lost and all is embraced. Now, in full awareness of what you are and from your realization of your essence, everything you need comes into your life without effort.

Willingness

You realize that this is a process that doesn't take place overnight or in the blink of an eye and therefore you are *willing* to do the work you need to do. Everyone you see or even think of is included in this Absolute Reality whether they consciously know it or not and whether or not their thoughts, words, and actions are in harmony with this Truth or not.

Intentional

Knowing that this is a process, you set the intention, every day if you must, to be what unconditional love calls you to *be* in this world. Setting this intention sends a crystal-clear message to ego that there is no turning back, that ego will never win, that Truth will always prevail, and that only Love is real.

Practice and Exercise

You allow intuition and inspired thought to guide you on your way. Nothing is forced as you allow this enlightenment process to take place. However, you realize that you can support this way of living and being by remaining vigilant. You can do this by engaging in practices and exercises that strengthen you. Simply spend time in silence asking Love to speak to you in ways you cannot possibly ignore, then listen for its nurturing guidance.

Always act on the inspiration you receive that you know is rooted and grounded in Love.

Now you have everything you need. No effort, no hard work, and no hours of study are needed. Just let the meditation of your heart remain focused on every eternal moment of Now, on what you are as Absolute Unconditional Love.

Symptom #7:

Concern About Personal Well-Being Has Decreased

As the concept of separation decreases you are released from individual needs and desires.

You have probably heard stories about Indian mystics sitting naked in caves high in the Himalayan mountains, or saints who deny themselves earthly comforts thinking it brings them closer to God. That is not what we are describing here. The need to deny yourself has disappeared, and it has also been simplified. You don't need to put a strain on the body or the mind, There is a need to release your attachments so that everything you really deserve can be given to you.

So what is it you really deserve? There is the answer ego-mind delivers, and then there is the quiet answer from your soul. Ego believes that you deserve riches, while the soul KNOWS that you deserve richness. Ego believes that you should be wealthy, while the soul KNOWS the importance of well-being. You hope and believe that all of these experiences can join as one, but there is a choice you must make first. Your concern about your personal well-being has blinded you to the universal well-being that is assured by God. Everything that is assured by God is true now and forever. The only thing left is for you to claim it for yourself

You may have noticed that we have returned to the difference between believing something and knowing EVERYTHING. You only know something to be true when you have had a direct experience of that truth. Until then your focus will be on belief, not certainty. One comes from the mind and the other comes from the soul. The goal of the mind is to understand what could never be understood, and this is the birthplace of mental confusion. The soul, on the other hand, knows Itself to be One with the Oneness of the universe, sometimes known as God. The need to understand this mentally has been replaced by a deeper knowing that the intellect will never grasp. Everything is included in this knowing, and this is what releases you from your individualized needs and desires. You have stepped into a universal space and the idea of personal well-being has vanished.

In the course of the awakening you are going through, a direct channel has been opened between the soul and the mind. In other words, you suddenly KNOW what has always been KNOWN and instantly SEE what has always been SEEN. Relax into this experience and it will continue to gain momentum, then you will realize that all of your questions have already been answered.

Are you confused at this point or are you beginning to experience greater clarity? This is the stage where we can do some evaluating. Your answers will tell you if you are still dancing between two worlds or have gained access to the world of ONE, sometimes known as Heaven; ego-based living and wanting or soul-based living and knowing. Whatever is coming up for you as you examine where you are in the awakening process will serve as a benchmark for you moving forward. As you spend some time in quiet contemplation, simply allow this to be a reference point showing you where you are along your path. Always keep in mind there is nothing you can force to happen, and you can only be where you are right now. Awakening is becoming aware of where you are

NOW and have always been, not a race to a non-existent finish line in the future.

It would serve you well to take a deeper dive with me into the opening paragraphs of this section. Clarity comes from wisdom and understanding which you always have access to. At times it may feel like wisdom and understanding are very elusive. At other times they feel like something you don't have but occasionally receive; like a flash of insight from something or from somewhere either inside or outside of you. However, wisdom and understanding are Divine capacities, attributes of the soul that you can tap into at any time. The struggle to comprehend something that is usually ego's point of observation where it relies only on input from the senses and past experiences.

Beyond ego's observation point there is the tower of the soul where wisdom and understanding show up in the form of *knowing*. There will always be that which is ineffable yet the enlightenment you experience will contain all wisdom, understanding, knowing, and a calm assurance of your own Divinity. For now, hold on to that word ALL. You will be coming back to it often. When you read and think of ALL, feel it as Whole. One. Holy. Sacred.

Divine. Complete. Everything. Everyone. Total. Absolute. Undivided. Peace. Harmony. Inclusive of ALL Good. ALL Love. ALL of God.

Let us dive deeper.

Detachment

Ego is always wanting. Always. It doesn't take a rocket scientist, a mystic, or a spiritually enlightened person to understand that if you want something it is because you are focused on not having that which you want. This is a ceaseless state of worldly consciousness that revolves around lack and not acknowledging that everything exists in the ALL that you are NOW.

As you move through your human experience it is only natural to want things. You inherently desire food, shelter, clothing, safety and security, loving relationships with others, peace, health and wholeness, and an abundance of all good things that make your involvement with life and living more joyful. Even in this section, you may be wanting more wisdom, understanding, and clarity.

Desires are not the problem. Your attachment to them is the issue. Attachments declare that this object or thing, circumstance, condition, situation, or event must be experienced in a certain way in order for you to feel happy, satisfied, whole, and complete. Your attachment is to the absence of the thing, plus the demand that it show up according to the guidelines you have established. It is important to remember that ego will never be satisfied because its natural state is fear. Its goal is self-preservation by perpetually looking to acquire things that represent what it thinks is missing. Its constant companion is a void and a feeling of incompletion. Ego is afraid this place will never be filled so it always wants more and feels that it deserves more.

Ego believes that you deserve riches, while the soul KNOWS that you deserve richness.

As ego continues to live in a constant state of fear its demand for *more* increases. More of anything, whatever it feels it lacks, and it feels that it lacks everything. This, in fact, is the foundation of ego's thought system. This feeling of being owed something that it perceives as missing, or lacking, is a symptom of error consciousness that has the potential to move you into playing the role of victim.

On the other hand, your soul knows that it is contained within the wholeness of God, one with the *ALL*. Your soul knows it already has access and shares in All things and nothing is missing. To deserve means to be worthy of. The soul, knowing that it is one of God, knows it is worthy of *ALL*, and that the gift has already been given. The soul knows that which is true for God is also true for the soul. Within this knowing is found *ALL* wisdom and understanding and you now begin to give birth to clarity and a more complete awakening.

The Divine Paradox – Certainty vs. Uncertainty

Ego needs the feeling of certainty to feel secure. It is certain that what it wants, which only represents something it feels is missing, will bring the security it longs for. It becomes attached to beliefs — most often unfounded beliefs — which become the foundation for its actions and behavior.

If you find yourself struggling with any of this perhaps it would be a good time to pause and examine your own beliefs. Where did your beliefs come from? Are they your beliefs or someone else's that you decided to go along with? Would changing your beliefs improve your life, improve the clarity and understanding that you are currently experiencing?

You will never be able to grow past the beliefs you cling to until you question their authenticity and relevance. Ego is a stubborn creature and believes it already knows everything it needs to prove its assertions. However, since its inherent nature is fear and insecurity, it may grant you some space to consider other options. Yet it clings to the need to be right and this is the only thing it is completely certain about.

You only know something to be true when you have had a direct experience of that truth. Until then focus will be on belief, not certainty.

God is *ALL*, Love is *ALL*, and everything that you could possibly want or desire is already contained within *ALL*. The soul is completely certain of this and this certainty is the single experience these chapters are leading you toward. The soul knows and is certain that everything is contained with this *ALLness*, and that is all it needs to know. It is not attached to anything else because *ALLness* is inclusive. The soul is not dependent on input from the senses. It is also not concerned with how its good will come, only that it is already here, and all its needs have already been met.

The soul is certain that whatever it focuses on will be fully realized. No attachment is necessary for this to be true. Ego, on the other hand, is constantly digging up the seed to see if it has begun to sprout. This *digging up* is meant to satisfy its attachment. Ego is attached to its desire that it ultimately takes root, ripens, and bears fruit. But it is this very attachment that prevents growth and pushes ego's desires further away.

Your universal well-being is assured by God

The intellect simply cannot comprehend All there IS. This is why the intellectual mind is limited and will never bring you to the goal of enlightenment. All cause and all effect proceed from the Divine. This is the Perfect Life of Spirit, and this is your life, this is *All*. When your thoughts are rooted and grounded in Perfect Life, Perfect Love, the Holy Sacred Goodness of God, which is Source and First Cause, and you finally awaken to the truth that this includes you, what shows up will always be supportive of your holy sacred life. This is your soul demonstrating, by out-picturing as an effect, the very richness of life that you have been called to experience.

Right beginning is essential to right ending. As you have already read, the beginning and the end is an illusion of measurement within the human construct of time. Outside of time, *right beginning* means the soul has always coexisted with *right ending* as a simultaneous experience of cause and effect.

> *"This simply means that from your human perspective, your beginning is the point of your awakening when your enlightenment moved you into an awareness of the infinite, eternal, divine flow where All is and where you realize and recognize your own divinity, yet you also know that you have been here all along".*

(See if your mind can wrap around that one.)

This is where you know that your well-being is assured by God and your human concerns are unnecessary.

You know this to be true because you have had a direct experience of the Omnipresence of God being your unfailing and all-providing Source of All good. And you also realize that you are one with the ALL and that within the *ALLness* of God you are also the Creator and the created in ONE. And yet, you did not create your Creator and thus experience yourself as an extension of the Divine. Here, in the energy of this knowing, you move about with a sense of Divine audacity. This boldness is not something that ego displays. It is a calm assurance that all is well with your Soul.

You make no claim for yourself that you would not also claim about God. What is true for God is true for you because you have been released from the concept of separation. Your ego may be shouting and crying sacrilege at this point in its last-ditch effort at self-preservation. You hear it not because you now know the truth of your own Beingness. The very power, glory, love, and wisdom that God is, is expressing as you, right here and right now. You are Divine!

By refusing to let ego, or anything you receive as input from the senses, speak in opposition to the truth you now know, you are beginning to shed the duality you have been experiencing up until now. Ego's voice begins to diminish. You now know what it means as you recall the instructions you received long ago:

"You shall have no other gods before or besides Me."

There is no such thing as God AND something else that has life, power, and substance. The Love that God *is* is all that is real and anything that would oppose this is born out of fear and is therefore unreal. As you direct your will to stay centered in this Truth, the illusion of the internal lower and higher nature, or ego and Soul, continues to fade into its native nothingness.

One is *All* there is. One Life is *All* there is. This One Life is God. This One Life is Love. This one Life is Good. This Life is your Life now. You are waking up. You are feeling Good and when you are feeling Good you are feeling God. Indeed, all is well with your Soul.

"Look at the birds of the air; they neither sow nor reap nor gather into barns, and yet your heavenly Father feeds them. Are you not of more value than they? And can any of you by worrying add a single hour to your span of life? And why do you worry about clothing? Consider the lilies of the field, how they grow; they neither toil nor spin, yet I tell you, even

Solomon in all his glory was not clothed like one of these." Matthew 6:26:30

Symptom #8:

Tenderness For All Beings

The desire to serve increases, including a sense of love and connection with the smallest and most vulnerable creatures.

The shift from ego consciousness to whole-mindedness is really the awakening of the heart of compassion. This usually shows up as a feeling of profound tenderness for all beings, which includes people, animals, insects, and every other type of creature. Each one becomes a living extension of the Divine and causing pain to any of them becomes almost unbearable. This is because the barrier that seems to separate one from another is in the process of dissolving. Ultimately, the compassion you feel for everyone is an extension of the compassion you are offering to yourself because you SEE yourself in every creature. All separating walls collapse in this experience, and at first, it may feel raw and uncomfortable, but as you adjust you will notice a quality of love penetrating your consciousness that you have never known before.

The need to serve others also increases during the awakening process. You realize that your highest purpose is to be truly helpful. This could mean many things, but it ultimately means assisting others, either directly or energetically, in their awakening, not so much through the words you say but the quality of the energy you transmit. St. Francis of Assisi once said:

"Our only job is to preach the gospel wherever we go, and to use words only when necessary."

He understood that words often get in the way and block the true experience that is needing to be shared. He also knew that the true teacher is the quality of love we share. This is what transforms at the highest level, inviting everyone we meet into the same awakened state that we are beginning to experience.

Serving others becomes the vehicle through which our awakening deepens and matures. All we want to do is give the gift that has been given to us, or to share that which has been shared so generously. You will likely find yourself volunteering for one cause or another, but you will

116

also realize that the real service has very little to do with the physical activity you are performing. The radiation of your awakened Self becomes the teacher as well as the teaching because you realize that in the end, you are giving only to yourself and serving the Beloved within each person.

When all of this becomes your everyday experience you will know what this symptom is truly indicating. Experiencing this will serve as confirmation that you have come down with a very desirable case of extreme chronic enlightenment. Congratulations!

This is one of the most beautiful experiences on your path to enlightenment. Knowing that nothing can be forced but simply a marker you arrive at one day. You wake up in the Light! You wake up knowing that beyond a shadow of a doubt, all that is Real is Love and all that is Love is God. You can never *not know* this again! This profound awareness of Love goes way beyond the subjective experience of Love and God. Now that you have arrived here, you cannot NOT see, feel, and experience this beautiful, potent power of Love in all life. Everywhere you turn you now see God as

Love living all life. You know this as Truth, not an idea or a concept of Truth but the real thing.

It is like stepping into a whole new world. You may even wonder "where has all this been hiding, how could I have missed this?" Overwhelming, staggering, astounding, and breathtaking all at the same time. You clearly see God as the animating Principle breathing all creatures. You drop to your knees in thanksgiving for the opening of your eyes. All life is God pressing out into visibility and this you behold with a tremendous sense of awe.

God is Life, God is Love, God is All and at this stage, this is your experience of Truth. You have moved past realizing that this Life is your life or your experience, to knowing this is true for all life. In every moment of every day, you find excitement and profound joy because you see the face of God everywhere you look, including in all creatures great and small.

Tenderness, warmth, gentleness, compassion, mercy, and grace, along with a greater sense of Love as Life, are now your constant companions as you see God dispensing Itself through so many forms. It is almost like God has been hiding in plain sight. Perhaps you were like one of the many who falsely thought and believed that they may only have a longshot chance, if any, at seeing God someday in a faraway place, and worse yet, not until after you die an earthly death. Now you know, really know, that nothing could be further from the Truth.

Right there in front of you, and all around you at the same time, you see God as Life and Love. In the kitten and goat, and in the grasshopper, gopher, and katydid. In the turtle and dog, and yes, even in the mouse and mosquito. God is everywhere present and you now stand in absolute awe at how infinitely spectacular your world has become. You are home and yet you know deep within that you have been here all along.

In all your excitement have you noticed that, once you arrived here, the once incessant voice of ego has been greatly diminished or perhaps even vanished altogether? This is one of the elements that make this place on your path so beautiful and really makes you feel like you have finally arrived. It has been an internal battle at times, hearing the ceaseless cries of ego. Up until now, it has continually craved attention and loudly voiced its desire to survive as the dominant player in the game of life. As darkness disappears whenever it is exposed to the light, the voice and fears of ego have also been silenced as they have been exposed to Love and Truth.

This has all come from your commitment to stay the course. Ego realizes that there is no way it can win and now knows it is powerless when it comes to Love and Life, Spirit, and Truth. Your ego knows its only chance for survival is to surrender, serve, and get on board. You can be sure there will be times it will let you know that it is still alive and well but with Love as your always-present travel companion, your ego will often be reminded that its place is in the back seat quietly enjoying the ride.

All Life Becomes a Living Extension of The Divine

I remember the first time I put on a pair of sunglasses with amber lenses. Everything looked different, sharper, more beautiful, and vibrantly alive. Since sunlight contains all the colors, some of them, especially the extreme edges of reds and blues, will make some objects seem a bit out of focus and foggy. What the amber lenses do is block certain elements of light allowing in only the colors that are easier on the eyes and help you focus. That is why your vision is so much sharper when you wear amber-tinted sunglasses.

Likewise, at this stage of your awakening, it is as if you have put on a new pair of lenses with a much-desired filter. All the life you encounter along your path is now seen as it truly is — an extension of the Divine.

Formerly you looked at life having been afflicted with "judging a book by its cover" syndrome. You moved about your environment making hundreds of thousands of split-second judgments throughout each moment of each day. Stop and really think about this for a moment. Your preconditioning had previously acted like a filter that either accepted or rejected everything you looked upon — every person, every animal, every insect.

Each stranger was a potential friend or foe filtered by likes and dislikes. Their looks, their dress, the shape of their eyes, the color of their skin, the tone of their voice, their opinions, beliefs, and more. All are instantly filtered in the blink of an eye through pre-established guidelines based on previous input from the world around you, then screened by ego. With no consideration of their essence and true nature, your internal bias mechanism either lifted the gate or slammed it shut.

You most likely had a similar operating system when it came to animals, insects, and other forms of life. Fight or flight. Fear and distress. Anxiety and apprehension. You perhaps perceived potential danger and harm where none existed. How powerful the imagination is. Each judgment reinforces false beliefs.

Stop again and give thanks that you are wearing your new glasses. Through the lens of enlightenment, everything is now properly filtered. What is false is no longer perceived. You see life as it truly is, the Divine pressing out. God as form. Love living the form you see as Life in all its variations. You are now seeing and experiencing Reality as opposed to what you previously thought was real. There is no fear and distress, only love and joy. Anxiety and apprehension have been replaced with warmth and tenderness. Any engagement with any form of life is now a holy and sacred experience as you know you are meeting God again yet for the very first time, and all is well with your Soul.

Awakening of the Heart of Compassion

The warmth and tenderness you now feel is really the unveiling of your true nature which is Love. The very essence of Love is kindheartedness, compassion, grace, and mercy. This is what you are beginning to feel now as you exchange energy with all life forms, all creatures great and small. You feel no sense of separation. The veil has been lifted. You experience a sense of harmlessness and harmony with all the life you now embrace along your way. Likewise, every form of Life is acknowledging you as One with God as you move through this field of experience we call life. Welcome to Heaven. You have been here all along and now you see it and KNOW it.

You Will Want to Serve

What God can do is done through you. This is the foundation of true service. You will intuitively know what is yours to do as you remember that the *doing is always in the being.* Your attention will not necessarily be focused on actions, yet you will act. This will often be the level of energy and the consciousness you maintain. Not all life sees through the same lens you now wear, yet all life will respond to the energy of light and love you are being. This is one of the highest ways you will be in service to life.

The Radiation of Your Awakened Self Becomes the Teacher

This is called Presence. You now model and demonstrate what it means to be enlightened by simply being your awakened self. You will not have to use words unless Love inspires you to speak. It is only the way of ego that says, "Look at me, I'm enlightened".

Your Light shines effortlessly and the Love you are causes ripples, just as a pebble does in a pond. Your illuminating presence has a magnetizing effect and life responds by being attracted to you. The unawakened life you encounter desires to experience the same joy-filled Light of Presence it sees and feels in you. All that is yours to do is to be the Light, to continue to shine. Not because other life has no light but to show all life that the Light in you is also in them.

This is another good spot for you to pause and do some reflection. Feel the intensity of this next statement and realize the responsibility that comes with it. Spend some quality time with this. Pray and consider the duty that comes with this realization:

You have been called and you have been chosen to be the Presence of God in this world.

Do you really understand this at the level of Soul? Are you now truly aware of your own Divinity?

Once you comprehend this beyond the level of the intellect, you will never be the same again. Prior to this moment of awakening, you may have used affirmations claiming this truth, repeating them mechanically but without any real feeling of your statements being true. At this stage of your enlightenment, you experience this as spiritual understanding and it may even feel as if your Soul, all that you are, has gone supernova. You may very well experience an emotional impact as you realize the profound magnitude of this Truth. You feel like your Divine brilliance has been magnified thousands of times, yet you remain humble and meek, gentle, and kind, always asking how you may serve. You seek ways to give God and be God, quietly and with spiritual strength, as you move along your path.

This is how it was meant to be. Breathe and relax. Let go and let God. You are not alone. Let this light shine upon every creature made by God, remembering that every creature is perfected within God.

Pray:

Show me how may I serve as the God in me meets the God in others and in all life?

Symptom #9:

Concrete Perceptual Thoughts Start to Fade

Your thoughts are becoming more abstract as the space between your thoughts increases

Don't become overly concerned if you realize that you are no longer able to string your perceptual thoughts together as quickly or as well as you once could. I often tell my students that the mind becoming like a sieve is a sign of enlightenment. For people who are accustomed to high intellectual processing, this can be very disconcerting in the beginning. Many will think that they are in the early stages of Alzheimer's or some other mental deficiency. Once again, don't worry about this at all. The best advice I can give is to simply roll with it. What does that mean? It is going to mean something different to each person, but the main thing is to relax and let go of your concern. Once again, this is a sign that the awakening is taking root and will soon begin producing good fruit.

Ego maintains its control by holding your thoughts together in a tight grip with very little space between each one. As you begin to wake up, the space between your words and thoughts begins to increase. This is the natural state of the soul, to open and initiate a new way of thinking and a new way of being. This new way is abstract instead of concrete. You will find yourself becoming quiet and yet your heart will open wider than you can imagine. Welcome this feeling, don't resist it no matter how uncomfortable it feels in the beginning. I promise it will subside soon.

As your heart continues to open at this stage of enlightenment, you will experience greater peace of mind. You will feel more awake and aware along with an overall sense of spaciousness which feels like a greater sense of freedom. This sensation is a very real part of your awakening and is also a result of the new way you are processing information. In the previous section, I shared that you may begin noticing ego's voice gradually fading away which continues here. Just relax and let it happen.

Ego is busy putting all its effort into trying to hold onto center stage as it bears witness to your spiritual unfoldment. It knows it is losing the battle.

Ego has its roots in the carnal world, therefore it finds it harder and harder to comprehend your ethereal and celestial thoughts which are much more predominant now. That would be like a child in pre-school attempting to participate in a debate regarding quantum mechanics with scientists and college professors. It makes no sense, so it sees no use in even trying.

Since you have also moved away from engaging with ego at every turn, and you no longer grant its wish to participate in moment-to-moment arguments that seem so silly to you now, you withdraw most of the power it previously received from you.

A very interesting phenomenon takes place as you continue to separate from ego's grasp. It occurs in the processing field of your thoughts and in what is taking place in your mind. Since you are no longer participating in an argumentative dialogue with ego, you free up a lot of what I call mental bandwidth or capacity. You have created an open mental and spiritual arena where you now have room to develop, or consciously choose not to develop, each thought you become aware of. This is what grants you the feeling of spaciousness and freedom.

Here is what is taking place in your mind, as explained in a very elementary way. Every day you think thoughts and a lot of them. Science has estimated that you have anywhere from forty to sixty thousand thoughts per day. Some experts say the number may be higher and some say it may be lower, but in either case, I am sure you agree that is a tremendous amount of thought being processed daily.

Every time you think a thought, immediately right after the thought, there is a space or a gap. Right after the gap, you have another thought, then another gap. And so it goes; on and on throughout your day. You have a thought, there is a gap. You have another thought, there is another gap, then another thought and another gap. Of course, this is all happening very quickly, perhaps every millisecond or even every nanosecond.

What normally takes place in this gap? A rapid-fire, split-second, decision-making activity. This is the processing your mind is doing all day every day. Your mind is working very, very, very quickly. Within each gap, you are deciding if you want to develop the thought you were just thinking about, abandon the thought, think more about it, or just put it aside for another time so you can move on and think another thought. There are actually an infinite number of options, and your mind is considering many of them at the same time.

What I find very interesting, and I think you will too, is that out of these forty to sixty thousand thoughts you are thinking every single day, most of them are the same exact thoughts you considered yesterday and probably the day before, even the day before that. Most of these thoughts are centered around a to-do list, worries, doubts, fears, assumptions, the past, the future, and anything else you allow ego to throw in there.

The good news is that something changes as you move along this path of awakening. This change is what you may be experiencing right now as you explore this particular symptom of enlightenment. As this thought-gap process continues, you not only become more aware of the gap but the gap increases in duration. You will notice there is more space between your thoughts, and you recognize this space as another field of infinite potential. In other words, the gap between your thoughts is increasing and offering you an opportunity.

You are becoming more and more aware of the power you have to continually choose. You know that ego no longer needs to be a primary influence. You begin to use these gaps in a more deliberate way. Not only do you notice that you are taking an active role as a vigilant gatekeeper of your thoughts and therefore your mind, but you are also being much more selective.

In this gap you are able to ask questions like:

"Is this thought holy, sacred and pure, born of love, supportive of love and all that is Real?"

"Is this thought in alignment with all I Am intending to be in this life experience?"

Or any other multitude of Divine Life and Love affirming questions. Each gap offers an opportunity to stay the course by asking the right questions and getting your Soul involved in this process. These gaps provide you with abundant fertile space to live life intentionally, a life that is in perfect harmony with the Love you are, the expression of God you are here and now.

At this point, you should be able to see and feel how your holy sacred self begins to take over as you fully awaken. You have become more aware of your spiritual power which sees to it that ego does not breach the gap in order to influence your thoughts. Behind the scenes, your spiritual power is being developed and as this happens, ego gives up the fight as it sees no way in or around.

Spend some time really contemplating this. Each step on this pathway of enlightenment should fill you with a sense of gratitude for the gifts they bring. In one way it is simply the awareness of the gap and the way this space between your thoughts is lasting longer and longer. That would be the perspective of the intellect and it would be easy to just move on. However, as you consider this from the perspective of your Soul, you should eventually see this gap for the extraordinary opportunity it brings. Think of this gap as spiritual soil. Rich in nutrients that will support anything you desire to plant. You get to decide what seeds you will scatter, and this will ultimately lead to the harvest you will soon enjoy.

What do you want your garden to look like? As you continue your awakening you will want to experience love growing everywhere, so that may be your first choice. Sprinkle love everywhere, in each and every gap. Remember, what takes place in each gap is leading you to your next thought, so sprinkle and plant wisely. Know that those thoughts are things and the thoughts you wrap with feelings and emotions move your *thought-idea* from the invisible world of non-form to the visible world of form by thought repetition and your consistent actions.

Fill your bag of seeds with all the aspects of the divine you want to experience in your life. Fill it with beauty and wisdom, peace and harmlessness, faith, and strength, understanding and humility, light and compassion, grace and mercy, respect, honor and integrity, purity and truth, and all that is praiseworthy. When you do this, you can be assured that each next thought will be born of love rooted and grounded in the Divine and all that is real.

I pray you now understand the power that you have been given with this gift. Whatever you continue to plant in these *thought-gaps* will eventually germinate, take root, then blossom and inhabit your garden, your life. You get to choose everything that grows in your garden. Isn't that amazing news? Use the power of your imagination and make it beautiful. Make it Heaven.

You must, however, continue to be vigilant and exercise a bit of caution as you become more and more aware of the power within these gaps. Just because you have explored this symptom and perhaps reached this stage of enlightenment, it doesn't mean it is not possible for weed seeds to get in your bag. Just like all the qualities of love and aspects of the divine you carry around as seeds for your garden, what you don't want can get into the bag as well. And just because ego has been expelled from the *gap*, doesn't mean it will not show signs of life and try to infiltrate the process every now and then.

Strive to stay awake and aware of what you are planting in these *gaps*. Weeds can look like worry, doubt, fear, anger, hostility, animosity, and even hatred. You don't want to plant selfishness, bitterness, and resentment in your garden either. You must understand that the gap will accept whatever seeds it is given without judgment, so it is up to you to deliberately design your garden with the fruit seeds of Spirit.

As you continue to become awakened more and more, the seed selection process becomes easier, even automatic. You will quickly identify the good seeds and just as quickly reject the weed seeds that show up. As you continue along your way, the frequency of their appearance will begin to diminish. Then one day you will look out at your enlightened garden with great joy and wonder. The tiny seeds you planted have become great trees bearing life-giving fruit, not only for you to enjoy but for everyone you touch.

With the absence of the tight knot of thoughts that were once so prevalent, you will also come to realize that not every spacious gap requires intentional planting. As you move along your path of enlightenment, your garden will produce the fruits of your thought seeds. You will enjoy the spaciousness you feel in these *gaps* and simply rest and enjoy the flowering. This is called *Practicing the Presence* while spending time in the silence. Your heart is opening wider and wider allowing you to feel deeply and more completely the Presence of God. As this increases and bliss overwhelms you, your knowing that only Love is real will be passionately fortified. You will know that you are home, the home you never actually left except in your imagination.

This is another good place to stop and breathe into the eternal moment of NOW. Perhaps you are still trying to wrap your intellectual mind around what is being described within this ninth symptom of enlightenment. Or perhaps you have found some assurance that you are on track. In either case or anywhere in between, pause and breathe. Take some time to see and feel the movement of Spirit — this magnificent gift of God you have found here — all contained in what was previously an unnoticed nanosecond (which is one billionth of a second, by the way).

Amazing, truly amazing when you consider how often you may have previously looked outside yourself for answers. Maybe you even found yourself gazing up at the stars searching for some extraordinary message, sign, or vision. Yet all along it has been right here in the gap, so easy to overlook. In these fleeting nanoseconds, you have been given the power to choose, the power to plant, and the power to ripen and bloom into the fullness of Love you are truly called to be.

Symptom #10:

The Need to Define the

Symptoms of Enlightenment

Disappears

The concept of unenlightened has fallen away, replaced by a feeling of unity and wholeness

The simplest way to explain the final symptom is that the barriers that once seemed to separate the ideas of enlightened from unenlightened, awake from asleep, have disappeared. This is the final stage in the awakening process, at least the final stage of this initial awakening. The idea that you were ever asleep has vanished and you realize, at the deepest part of your being, that reality was never compromised by your sleeping mind, and that the truth of who you are has remained a constant and continual opening to grace.

Read that last sentence again:

"The idea that you were ever asleep has vanished and you realize, at the deepest part of your being, that reality was never compromised by your sleeping mind, and that the truth of who you are has remained a constant and continual opening to grace."

Once this is realized, the need to define anything disappears completely. It vanishes because any definition requires separation, and this is impossible for you now. You are suddenly filled with a sense of unity and wholeness that evades the intellectual mind completely. You will still know how to interact with people in appropriate ways but you are not fooled into believing that they are anything more than the final images of the final dream. And you will celebrate this rather than regret anything that ever happened in your life.

Guilt and regret have finally given way to freedom and love. Forgiveness is now a fully realized, all-encompassing knowingness that you extend to all beings, certain that this is their destiny as well as yours.

Imagine spending your entire life with your eyes closed. It doesn't matter why you chose this or what purpose it served, only that you have been walking through the world unable to see what is right in front of you. Then one day something changes. For some reason, you realize that the need to keep your eyes closed has vanished and your eyelids finally begin to part. The world suddenly appears before you. All the things you felt with your hands or heard with your ears make total sense now. You are able to see clearly that which has always been so clear.

This is the process you are going through now. Nothing changes in the Real World, but you are suddenly able to see and experience that changelessness directly. You realize that you never actually left Heaven, though you chose, for one reason or another, to deny that fact and kept your eyes closed to the holy visions surrounding you. Guilt has dissolved and you realize that forgiveness was never even required. All definitions disappear in this light, including the definitions you placed upon yourself. You are able to See as God Sees and Know what God Knows, which is simply this: you are the holy perfect child of a holy perfect creator, unchangeable and secure in eternity's grasp. All dark shadows have disappeared, and you stand fully revealed in unending brightness. This is who you are and will forever remain, and the same is true for all.

Awareness

Let us take a deeper dive and explore this beyond the constraints of intellect and logic. The reason you no longer sense a barrier separating your ideas about being awake or asleep, enlightened or unenlightened, is because you have allowed them to dissolve. Actually, it is not the barriers that have dissolved but the realization that the barriers you perceived were never real. What has increased, expanded, and developed is your awareness. The veil has vanished since you now see everything as an integral part of ALL THAT IS.

It is like looking through the eye of a needle, believing you see the whole world, and calling that which you see reality or the whole world. As the curtain of separation dissolves your awareness broadens. You now see so much more than you could ever take in through just the eye of the needle. You are also able to *SEE* using much more than your physical eyes. You are now seeing with your intuition, inspired thought, innate divine knowledge, and the wisdom of your Soul which is fully aware of its own divinity. This is Perfect Vision. You are now seeing through the lens of what you are Feeling (with a capital F instead of a small f) and you are fully aware of your holy sacred Self. You now see and feel Truth and Ultimate Reality.

You now see *All* and the *All* that you see is that which is truly Real, that which is truly Love. Your awareness takes in the whole, sees the whole, feels the whole, and beyond the logical mind, understands how it all comes together as One.

Even though you may have labeled your previous state of conscious awareness as being asleep, it too has been an essential component of this *whole* you are aware of now. It matters not what you stamped as being awake or asleep, enlightened or unenlightened, aware or unaware because from this vantage point you now know that every experience provided the necessary contrast for you to recognize Truth, and to be fully aware of all that is *Real*.

You exist, just as you have always existed, within the Omnipresence God. This is your Truth and this Truth never changes. It is the same today, yesterday, always, and forever. And this is the same Truth for all people, all life, and for all times and in all places. There is no place where you can go or be where God is not. There is no place where you can go or be where this is not true.

It is as if you stepped into Heaven only to realize that you have always been here, or that you never left. Every previous experience has contributed to your expanded awareness. What is yours to do is simply be grateful that you are now, have always been, and will always be, in the flow of God's Grace. That is why you are here, awake and aware, in this eternal moment of now.

Perspective

You have also made a shift in your perspective and this is why definitions are no longer necessary. You see everything as it truly is, through the lens of Truth and Love, and you know what you perceive without having to wonder "What is that?" You simply See what you See and Know what you Know, without filters and without distinctions. Quite simply, everything you perceive is ONE, and the need to separate, define or clarify that Oneness has completely disappeared.

Notice how you feel now that you have fully embraced this experience of Oneness. Feeling is the secret to keeping your Soul anchored in God. Your Soul never forgot that Heaven is your Home. Your feeling of God's Omnipresence (which is also yours) assures you that your Soul is forever wrapped in Divine Love. This is the greatest freedom you have ever experienced because you now feel the full spectrum of this unconditional Love. Remorse, shame, and the need to attack no longer dwell within you. You can see how they have been transformed from the temporary into a greater understanding of the many dimensions of Love. All the former feelings of guilt and regret are now viewed for what they were — a call to return home and know that only Love is Real. Knowing this, everything that is unreal vanishes on its own.

Think about your human vision for a moment. If you were to go to an empty field or a large body of water where your field of vision is unobstructed by buildings, trees, and other objects, how far would you be able to see? You would be able to see as far as the horizon. What you see appears to be all there is. However, you know the horizon is an illusion. If you walked toward it you would never get there. But if you believed what the whole world believed a few hundreds of years ago, you would be afraid that walking too far might mean your death, that you might fall off the edge. For that fear to dissolve you would need to experience what lies beyond the horizon. You would need to have a direct experience.

Having arrived here, as if beyond the horizon, fully awake and enlightened, yet knowing you have actually been here all along, grants you the full experience of unconditional love which brings with it an inner knowing that all is well with your Soul. This is why you will not find it necessary to define anything and you now consider it absurd to criticize all the things you perceived as a mistake or a character fault. You have finally grasped at a level beyond the intellect what the unconditional in unconditional love truly means.

Understanding

Within the experience of unity and wholeness, all is understood beyond what the intellect is capable of understanding. This is called spiritual understanding. Spiritual understanding comes as a revelation directly from Spirit to the mind. Spiritual understanding does not rely on the individual's supplements of knowledge and intelligence. It is a direct download from the Divine and is uncompromised in every way.

Until now you have come to know that God is the energy of Love that is not only Omnipresent but is also that Presence that is Omniscient and Omnipotent. The Omniscience that is God is infinite intelligence, knowledge, and wisdom which is always available to you. There is nothing unknown for you to fear or be concerned over. Within the Omnipotence that is God, all the power that ever was, is, and will be is yours now and forever.

Having come to this place where you have finally moved beyond belief to knowing, you find no need to make any false claims for yourself that you would not make for God. You see with clarity all that is Real and the unreal fades from your sight and your experience. This is the wholeness and the feeling of ultimate liberty that comes from spiritual understanding.

Order

It has often been said that order is heaven's first law, and you clearly understand what that means here in this final stage. Even the intellect and logical mind join in this realization. Order brought you here through all the experiences that took place prior to this moment. Experiencing contrast was an absolutely indispensable part of the process of awakening. Without the experiences you have labeled as negative or even bad, how would you have known that there is something to wake up to? Even those who have gone through life without terrible trauma have noticed an inner longing and discontent for something more. No matter what the circumstances of life bring, we are all aware of an inner knowing or a ceaseless nudging that there is much more than our senses allow us to perceive.

Look around you and you will see that order is readily apparent in science, math, and astronomy. Divine Order will continue to serve you well as you continue on your enlightened path. Orderly thought brings feelings, then experiences that are in alignment and harmony with each other. As you acknowledge the Truth of the following statement, you can expect these Truths to be self-evident in your awakened experience:

"I Am the holy sacred presence of God, of Love, of Light, of Peace, of Wisdom, of Grace and Compassion,"

Order is also at work as law. It is important to remain attentive to the thoughts you are thinking and wrapping them with feelings and emotions. Divine law and order are impersonal and operate the same for All. Should you drift away from thoughts of Truth you may experience periods of being off and out of alignment. No need to be alarmed since this is simply Divine law and order calling you to course correct. You make this adjustment by renewing your mind. This is done by remembering you already know your Truth, that you are Divine.

Will

An awareness of will should be mentioned here. In this final stage of enlightenment, will is about maintaining focus, and your will to remain awake. Before arriving at this point, ego and intellectual mind would debate about whether your desires are the will of God or not. You now know that you could not have a will that would be separate from God's will because separation from God's will is impossible. Will becomes that which drives you. Your will is the thirst for spiritual nourishment that keeps you centered in the Light of Truth. God as Love is pressing out into visibility as you and through you. This is God's will and Love's way or there would be no need for any of this.

Sensitivity

In this fully awakened state, your compassionate heart is fully open to all beings in every circumstance. Your will is to be truly helpful and to always seek ways to help alleviate suffering. Sustaining thoughts aligned with Truth and speaking words fragrant with love is not enough. You know you must live the Truth you know. You continue to move along your way noticing what you are noticing with a heightened state of sensitivity. This is another way you see without relying solely on your eyes and other senses. Instead of moving along, looking the other way, and avoiding the pain and suffering of others, you seek ways to serve, knowing that you are always serving the God within each one. Love leads the way and as you act on the wisdom, inspiration, and guidance you receive, you notice your light becoming brighter and brighter.

Gratitude

It would be impossible to say too much about the importance of gratitude, appreciation, praise, and blessings. In this final stage, these become a natural extension of who you are, not just the actions you take. You fully experience the essence of this truth. Every moment of every day becomes a perpetual prayer of gratitude for the life you live and the givingness of God. Truly you have arrived in heaven, or the experience of heaven you never really left, wide awake, enlightened, and in all your glory, ceaselessly proclaiming:

"I AM That NOW and FOREVER!"

You're Not Going Crazy, You're Waking Up!

Well, there you have it. Now you can relax and allow your newly awakened consciousness to emerge and bless the world. I can't tell you how many people have struggled with these "symptoms" thinking there was something wrong with them. Maybe the ideas and activities that once meant so much to them have lost their meaning, or perhaps the space between their thoughts increased to the point where their minds felt like sieves. This list could have been much longer and perhaps there are several other symptoms you could add. All I can say is that the number doesn't matter.

The only thing that matters is NOW because this is where the awakening takes place. You are leaving the "then" and the "when" that creates so much confusion and entering into the eternal moment where you are already awake, already enlightened, and already whole. Don't worry about any of it. You are now and will always be in the perfect hands of a Perfect God. So relax, and let everything fall into place.

Let me give you one more indication that will tell you you are on the right track. You could say that it is the final symptom, perhaps the most important one. When this realization dawns you will know you are nearly home:

It is not you who is insane, but the world you live in.

Until now this may have been an impossible pill to swallow. Of course, many, many things in the world are challenging and polarizing. But insane? There are nice people in the world. Yes? There are beautiful places we can visit. Yes? So how is it that the world itself is insane?

It might be more helpful to say that the way we interact with the world is insane. We are not talking about the planet Earth, but the world of ego, the split-mind, that thinks only of its own needs at the expense of the needs of others. All one needs to do is look at the political environment in most countries. It is the same story we have been playing out for thousands of years — taking power for the sake of power, and doing whatever one can do to hold onto that power once it has been achieved. This is the world we live in, but it is not the world of the Soul which you are entering now.

It is time to look clearly at the world you created in your imagination to hide from reality. By now that statement should not seem so foreign or shocking. The world you think you see is not the real world. There is a world beyond this one that is wholly beyond the carnage of this place. You have been led to believe that millions of people being slaughtered for their religious beliefs, or millions more starving though there is plenty of food to feed the entire planet, is just the way of the world. Yes, the way of an insane world. But now your eyes are clear and you can see and consider what was impossible to consider before. Once again, it is not you who is insane, but the world you seem to live in.

So what can YOU do about all this?

It's quite simple, and you probably already know the answer — Wake Up. There is nothing this world needs more than awakened beings who live from the Soul, extending love wherever they go. People everywhere are feeling ego's dominance fade, but it will definitely *not* "go softly into that good night". Ego or split-mind will fight with all its might, and that is why things seem to be getting bleaker with each passing year.

This is how it works — it is always darkest before dawn. Your light and energy are required to enable the shift from fear to love, and from an insane world into one dominated by compassion and peace. So once again — Wake Up. You chose to be here before time began because you knew that this was the great moment of awakening, and that time as we have known it is about to end.

Time will end in light, not darkness. It is through you and everyone who sees past the façade of this make-believe world that a new world will come into being. It is happening right now. All we need to do is open our eyes, claim Heaven as our home, and step with confidence through the door.

If not now - when?

About the Authors

Fr. James F. Twyman, CFC, is an Episcopal/ Anglican priest and a Franciscan brother in The Community of Francis and Clare. He has published over 20 books including the NY Times bestseller The Moses Code, has directed or produced seven feature films including the award-winning Redwood Highway and Indigo, and has recorded nearly 20 music CDs. Known internationally as The Peace Troubadour, James has traveled to countries at war to perform The Peace Concert for over 25 years. During many of these peace journeys, he called people from around the world to pray and meditate for peace during World Synchronized Meditations. In some cases, millions of people participated in these meditations. James is also the founder and spiritual leader of Namaste Village, a nondual interfaith community in Ajijic, Mexico.

For more information about Fr. James, go to www.worldpeacepulse.com. For more information about Namaste Village, go to www.Namaste-Village.com.

About the Authors

Dr. Stephen J. Kosmyna, Ph.D. is an Elite Level Success and Mindset Consultant, an Inspirational Speaker, Prosperity Teacher, Trainer, Author, Coach, Spiritual Leader, Entrepreneurial Adviser, Metaphysician, and an Ordained New Thought Minister with Unity, The International Metaphysical Ministry and Divine Science. He provides inspiration, motivation, guidance, and coaching to individuals, small businesses, and corporations through an abundance of programs and workshops that cultivate radical personal and professional transformation, quantum leap goal achievement, and meditation and mindfulness practices. Dr. Stephen has a bachelor's and master's degree in Metaphysical Science with a focus on the subconscious mind and visualization, and a Doctor of Philosophy, Ph.D., in Holistic Life Coaching. He is also the voice of the human potential development podcast, The Genesis Frequency.

For more information go to Stephen@SuccessOcean.com.

77496035R00095